Jaguar XK8 and XKR

JAGUAR
XK8 and XKR

Plus XK180 and F-type Concept

John Blunsden

MOTOR RACING PUBLICATIONS LTD
Unit 6, The Pilton Estate, 46 Pitlake, Croydon CR0 3RY, England

First published 2000

British Library Cataloguing in Publication Data

Blunsden, John
    Jaguar XK8 and XKR : plus XK180 and F-type concept
    1. Jaguar XK automobiles
    I. Title
    629.2'222

ISBN 1899870 53 9

Typesetting and origination by Andrews-Empson Design, Croydon, Surrey

Printed in Great Britain by The Amadeus Press Ltd, Cleckheaton, West Yorkshire

Contents

Introduction and acknowledgements

To anyone who was once the owner of a Jaguar XJ-S (it was one of the V12 HE models, so the hyphen was still in place), the arrival of the XK8 had to be an important occasion. The earlier car, as its ultimate sales success confirmed, had many virtues as well as quite a few shortcomings, but certainly it was no real successor to the E-type, and for this I was most grateful, for the revered 'E', with its claustrophobic cockpit and minimal luggage space, would have been completely impractical for the use to which I would have had to put it.

Even the XJ-S, enjoyable as it was to drive, also proved to be an inadequate load carrier – as of course I always knew it would (it was a case of the heart having ruled the head) – so after a year or so it had to go. But I still retain many fond memories of that car, notably the effortless performance from the refined power of its monster engine – though not of its considerable thirst, which even

during an era of sensible fuel prices was something of a concern.

So my earnest hope when, after a few false starts, it was clear that the XK8 was finally on its way into production, was that this would be a car which retained all of the traditional Jaguar values of luxury, performance, refinement and style, but which could marry them to new standards of engineering integrity, manufacturing quality and affordability of ownership. In the course of researching this book it has become clear to me that all of this has largely been achieved.

Without exception, owners of XK8s and XKRs to whom I have talked have not been disappointed by their choice of car, and the message that invariably comes across is that it has grown on them, that the further they drive it the more they seem to like it. This was certainly my own experience with the XK8 Coupe and XKR Convertible which

Jaguar Cars kindly loaned to me for assessment and photography.

As will be seen from the sales figures quoted at the back of this book, Coupes have been favoured in the UK and Convertibles in the USA, the latter being the XK8 and XKR's largest single market. But this probably says more about the respective countries' weather patterns than indicating any conflict in the perceived quality of the two alternative body styles. Certainly the extra structural rigidity and additional space offered by the Coupe would probably have influenced my own choice for the UK had it been put to the test.

In addition to the aforementioned owners, and to some of the key figures who saw the car through into production and with whom I was able to have valuable conversations, I am most grateful for the generous support I have also received from Jaguar Cars' hard-worked Communications & Public Affairs staff, in particular to Sandy Angus and Claire Ellis and their respective colleagues, who provided me with important photographic material, statistical data and test facilities.

My aim in writing this book has been not only to explain in some detail the various models in the latest XK range – and to take a glance at what is still to come – but also to place these cars into the context of the total XK story, which veered off into XJ territory and has now returned. In particular, I hope the book will prove a valuable reference for anyone who is contemplating the purchase of a previously used XK8 or XKR and who needs to confirm the specification of the car or cars on offer. Whichever model is chosen, provided it has been properly cared for and serviced regularly, I feel sure that it will continue to give many thousands of miles of sheer enjoyment.

JOHN BLUNSDEN
October 2000

Five pillars of Jaguar's sports car heritage. The prewar SS100 began it all, but it was the XK120 roadster which stunned the world on its debut in 1948, followed by the E-type in 1961. The XJS was a controversial departure, but it had matured into a desirable GT car long before this Convertible arrived in 1994, setting the scene for the XK8, in the foreground, which was to combine the best features of its predecessors in a thoroughly modern package.

The XK story can also be divided into five chapters. The XK120, parked behind the XKR in the foreground, rewrote the definition of a modern sports car in 1948, then gave way to the more powerful and better equipped XK140 in 1954, which in turn led to the more bulbous disc-braked XK150 in 1957. Parked in front of it here is its contemporary, the D-type based XK SS, the rarest of all XK road cars, only 16 of which were to be built before a factory fire halted production.

CHAPTER 1

BUILDING THE XK LINE

Heritage of Jaguar sports cars

It is widely accepted that the Jaguar XK8 story began either in 1978 – the year when serious consideration was first given to the type of car which eventually would replace the XJS – or in 1992 – when the definitive shape of the XK8 was finally agreed after a whole rash of alternative proposals had been committed to the sketch pad and modeller's clay, ultimately for them to be discarded. Or some might argue that the starting date was late-1993, for only then was final approval given by Jaguar's new owners, the Ford Motor Company, for what had become known internally as the X100 programme.

But the story of the flagship car which has led Jaguar into the 21st Century really began very much earlier than that, in fact several years before the 20th Century had even reached its mid-point. For XK8 is just the latest chapter of the total XK story, which began incongruously at the height of the blitz during the early part of the Second World War.

The SS Jaguar factory in Browns Lane, Coventry was a prime target of the Luftwaffe bomber crews who visited Britain's industrial Midlands regularly from 1940 onwards, and senior executives would take their turn as members of the company's fire-watching team who would assemble on site every night with the hope of extinguishing any incendiary bombs which might fall on the premises.

Those who were not actually on the roof as look-outs would congregate in a small office in the development department and 'talk shop', and the company's founder, William Lyons – never slow to maximize an opportunity – ensured that the talk was of a constructive nature and specifically relevant to the resumption of car production after the war.

Bill Lyons had already come a long way since setting out as a manufacturer of stylish Swallow sidecars for motorcycles in modest premises in Blackpool (a seaside resort more famous today in motor industry circles as the home of TVR). From sidecars it had been a natural progression to craft attractive special Swallow bodies on to other car manufacturers' chassis, an activity which was to prove so successful that a move to larger premises and a bigger labour pool in Coventry had become necessary in 1928. The coachbuilding business in turn had led to the production of the first complete cars to be

---

Jaguar name synonymous with value and elegance

---

marketed under the SS name in 1931.

The Jaguar appellation had first been appended to a range of saloon cars introduced in 1935 which were remarkable not only for their competitive price but also – like almost every product that had ever left the company's premises – their elegant lines,

A production Jaguar sports car that might have been. This was a 1938 prototype coupe based on the SS Jaguar 100 chassis, but the approaching Second World War put paid to any thoughts of putting the car into production.

for Lyons was already firmly established as a man with a brilliant eye for style, elegance and attention to detail. This new range had set the tone for the company's products right through to 1939, when production was halted by the war, and it was clear during those war years that the models which had been earmarked for 1940 would have to form the initial product range when car manufacture resumed.

Largest model creates need for in-house engine

But replacement models were already in the planning stage, and they were to include the largest model the company had yet produced – a saloon (sedan) specifically aimed at the US market, to which British manufacturers would have to export the bulk of their production in order to qualify for

steel supplies at a time of desperate shortage. The need adequately to power this car (the Mk VII) reinforced Lyons' determination to remove the one remaining impediment to the future growth and prosperity of his company – the lack of an in-house engine. Hitherto, SS cars (the initials were believed by some to stand for Swallow Special and by others for Standard Swallow) had been powered by engines bought from the Standard Motor Company (later to be merged with and eventually submerged by Triumph). Not only was there uncertainty about future supplies from this source, but the Standard engines, even after attention by the tuning expert and gasflow specialist Harry Weslake, had limited longer-term potential.

But Lyons wanted much more than 'just' a Jaguar-designed and built engine; it had to be one which produced a significantly higher level of performance than any existing volume-produced power unit of its size, a target output being set at 160bhp, which was deemed the minimum necessary to give the projected Mk VII the required top speed of 100mph. Equally important to someone with such a highly tuned aesthetic sense, it had to be visually the most attractive engine on the market, so that lifting the bonnet (hood) would evoke gasps of admiration to rival those generated by the cars' external lines and interior decor.

Such was the brief which Bill Lyons gave to three of his nocturnal fire-watchers – William Heynes, his chief engineer, and two of his key members of staff, Walter (Wally) Hassan and the recently recruited Claude Baily. The outcome, which has rightly been recorded as the most important milestone in Jaguar history, was the conception and creation of the famous twin-overhead-camshaft engine, different versions of which were studied under a variety of codenames from XE to XJ before the definitive six-cylinder power unit (initially in 3.4-litre form) appeared under the name XK.

Much of the initial development work took place while the war was still on, which meant that the engine was ready for production by 1948, but unfortunately the Mk VII for which it was intended was still anything up to two years away because of the lead time for the production of bodies, which for the first time in the company's history had to be out-sourced. In the meantime, an interim model, the Mk V, had been slipped into the schedule, which married the chassis and torsion-bar independent front suspension which had been developed for the Mk VII with the Weslake-modified but Standard-sourced 2½-litre and 3½-litre engines, hidden beneath bodywork which still had much in common with that of the last prewar SS Jaguars, which as a temporary measure had been brought back into production under the Jaguar name.

There was no question of re-engineering the Mk V to take the XK engine because the car would be withdrawn from production when the Mk VII arrived in 1950, so the decision was taken to make a shorter version of the new chassis, drop the XK engine and a suitable driveline into it and clothe it with an open two-seater body. Not only would it give the company an additional model line, it would be a useful way of testing the performance and reliability of the new engine and eliminating any 'bugs' that might be revealed before it was installed in the Mk VII.

The company was not new to sports cars, of course, and the SS90 and SS100 had earned a considerable name for themselves before the war with their classic (long-bonnet, short-tail) lines and impressive performance, but they had been a very low-volume line (hence the decision not to bring them back into series production after the war), and the thinking at Browns Lane was that a new two-seater, too, would find only a limited market. The plan, therefore, was to

The car which began the XK story, the original XK120 roadster which took Earls Court by storm in 1948.

The XK140 of 1954 was a logical development of the XK120 with more power, more comfort, rack-and-pinion steering and exposed rear wheels to assist brake cooling.

prepare for a short production run of around 200 cars, which would be assembled with aluminium-panelled bodywork.

It is a well-recorded part of Jaguar history, of course, that the new car – called the XK120 as an indication of its potential top speed – became the sensation of the 1948 Earls Court Motor Show, when it shared the Jaguar stand with the new Mk Vs. The combination of superbly elegant lines and the prospect of a vivid performance with what appeared at the time to be a ludicrously low price of £998 was sufficient for hundreds of car-starved enthusiasts to rush for their cheque books (not that there was much likelihood of obtaining delivery for a very long time).

Any thoughts that the XK120 would be a limited-production model were soon abandoned and the car had to be retooled for steel bodywork. The open two-seater, which had gone into series production in July 1949, was joined by a fixed head coupe in March 1951 and a drophead-coupe in April 1953, and by the time the XK120 was replaced by the XK140 in October 1954 over 12,000 had been built – 60 times the original estimate. They included Special Equipment versions with a higher-compression engine giving an additional 20bhp and uprated suspension, which became an essential starting point for

anyone indulging in motorsport.

By the time the XK140 came along Jaguar had been making big headlines in the sport, initially with the XK120 in international rallies and production car racing, but more especially in endurance racing with a purpose-built derivative based on a tubular chassis, the XK-C, or C-type as this charismatic model became known. Built specifically for the 1951 24-hours race at Le Mans, after a specially prepared XK120 had finished second there the previous year, the C-type took a convincing outright victory on its debut, then repeated its success in 1953 with disc-braked examples of the same model.

Continuing to build on their growing Le Mans legend, the factory returned in 1954 with an all-new monocoque-constructed racer, the famous D-type, and although that year they lost out by less than 2 minutes to a victorious Ferrari, the D-type strung together three victories in a row from 1955 to 1957, the last year finishing 1st, 2nd, 3rd, 4th and 6th, led by cars operated by Ecurie Ecosse, the Scottish team whose own D-types had previously supplemented the works entries, and who took over the lead role following the factory's withdrawal from direct participation in racing at the end of the 1956 season.

The magnificent C-type, the car which made Jaguar a victor at Le Mans for the first time in 1951, then went back there two years later with disc brakes to repeat the success.

The D-type, a triple Le Mans winner in 1955-57 and an equally brilliant long-distance racer elsewhere, marked the pinnacle of Jaguar's racing achievements during the Fifties.

Meanwhile, on the roads the XK140 was seen as the logical development of the XK120, with revised rear suspension, rack-and-pinion in place of recirculating-ball steering and maximum power of the standard engine increased from the 160bhp of the XK120 to 190bhp with, as previously, a further 20bhp available with the optional Special Equipment specification, which included C-type cylinder heads. As with its predecessor, three body styles became available, the open two-seater remaining the most popular of the trio, and altogether almost 8,900 cars were to be built and sold before the XK140 in turn gave way to the XK150 in March 1957.

This was a more radical change, the new car having cleverly reprofiled bodywork fronted by a lower and broader radiator grille, and there was the welcome adoption of disc brakes all round, the inadequate drum brakes having been the weakest point of both the earlier series, and within a few months of the car's launch automatic transmission became available on an XK Jaguar for the first time. Another new option was an S-specification engine with Weslake-developed cylinder heads and triple carburettors, which helped to boost power to 250bhp.

At first, the XK150 was available only as a fixed-head or a drop-head coupe, the open two-seater version being added a year later, but when this third variant arrived it came with the option of a larger-bore engine, bringing the capacity up to 3.8 litres and a maximum output of 220bhp in standard form or 265bhp with the triple-carburettor set-up. Later the larger engine was also offered with the other two body styles, and this time it was the fixed-head coupe which proved the most popular version, accounting for almost half of the total output of nearly 9,400 XK150 and XK150S models. This was partly explained by the fact that the closed car was also the longest lived of the trio, for whereas production of both the open variants ceased in October 1960, the fixed-head coupe continued to be available for a further 12 months. By that time, however, another XK two-seater coupe was making all the headlines.

The original XK120 having already spawned two further generations of sports Jaguars, it was not surprising that even at the launch of the XK150 it had become clear that this would have to be the final

When the XKs went to Le Mans

No sooner had the first XK-engined cars – the production version of the original aluminium-panelled XK120s – been driven off the production line at Browns Lane than they were appearing on the race tracks, and what better public debut than in the hour-long race for standard production cars which supported the main event at the first *Daily Express* International Trophy meeting at Silverstone in August 1949, when Leslie Johnson chalked up the first of the XK120's many wins.

But it was under the unique Le Mans spotlight that the XK's racing legend really took shape and where Jaguar's factory participation in motorsport was to be most impressively rewarded. It all began when a trio of XK120s were entered in 1950, one of which, shared by Leslie Johnson and Bert Hadley, challenged for the lead before retiring, while the other two finished 12th and 15th of the 29 survivors. But things would get a great deal better. Such was the importance of Le Mans that purpose-built cars were designed and developed for this and other international endurance races – the famous C-type and its successor, the D-type. Here is a summary of the successes achieved by these factory-entered or supported XK-powered cars in the annual 24-hour race:

1951
Jaguar C-type   P Walker/P Whitehead 1st
1953
Jaguar C-type   D Hamilton/A P R Rolt 1st
Jaguar C-type   S Moss/P Walker 2nd
Jaguar C-type   P Whitehead/J Stewart 4th
1954
Jaguar D-type   D Hamilton/A P R Rolt 2nd
Jaguar C-type   J Swaters/R Laurent 4th
1955
Jaguar D-type   M Hawthorn/I Bueb 1st
Jaguar D-type   J Claes/J Swaters 3rd
1956
Jaguar D-type   R Flockhart/N Sanderson 1st
Jaguar D-type   J Swaters/F Rousselle 4th
1957
Jaguar D-type   R Flockhart/I Bueb 1st
Jaguar D-type   N Sanderson/J Lawrence 2nd
Jaguar D-type   J Lucas/J-M Brussin 3rd
Jaguar D-type   P Frere/F Rousselle 4th
Jaguar D-type   D Hamilton/M Gregory 6th

The original XK120 concept was approaching its 10th anniversary when this final variant, the XK150, with its wider and more roomy body, disc brakes and optional 3.8-litre engine, appeared in 1958.

derivation of the original design. In fact, some initial modelling work on the sort of car which might ultimately replace it had begun around the time when the first XK140s had arrived in the showrooms, although it was not until 1957 that the first clues appeared as to precisely what the next Jaguar sports model might look like.

The previous year, works driver Duncan Hamilton had equipped his 1954 D-type – the car with which he and co-driver Tony Rolt (who had shared the winning C-type at Le Mans in 1953) had chased the winning Ferrari so closely on their return to Le Mans that year – with a full windscreen for road use, and in doing so he sparked off the thought that a limited-production road version of the car might be saleable. There was an adequate supply of parts on tap at Coventry, so during the winter of 1956/57 the decision was taken to begin a short production run of a road-equipped D-type, the resulting car being given the designation XK SS. Unfortunately, only 16 of them had been completed when, during one night in February 1957, a disastrous fire destroyed much of the Jaguar factory and with it all the remaining XK SS body tooling and components.

Of course, this could never have been a mainstream model, but the car which *would* eventually replace the XK150 also had a link with the Le Mans race, albeit only a brief one. Briggs Cunningham, an American 'regular' at Le Mans with cars bearing his own name, arrived for the traditional test weekend in 1960, not with another Cunningham, but with an experimental Jaguar. Lent to him by the factory, prototype E2A was an indication of the sort of car that Jaguar themselves might well one day be racing should they decide to return to the tracks. There was quite a lot of 'D-type' in its beautifully

---

Malcolm Sayers' brilliance on display again at Le Mans

---

smooth lines, which one might have expected from the brilliantly gifted Malcolm Sayer, who had also been responsible for the D-type's graceful, elegant and aerodynamically efficient shape. But the most significant development beneath the skin of E2A was its completely independent rear suspension with fixed-length drive-shafts, lower wishbones

Racer on the road. The XK SS was a novel conversion of the D-type into a street-legal two-seater and might have been more plentiful but for that factory fire in 1957.

and twin co-axial coil spring/damper units, and with disc brakes inboard-mounted adjacent to the differential housing.

Unfortunately, an early problem with the car's fuel-injection system led eventually to its retirement well before half-distance, but perhaps of more significance was the other prototype, E1A, which was still back at the factory in Coventry. It had been built in 1958 to test components intended for Jaguar's next production sports car, including that independent rear end. By the following year, the first full-size pre-production open two-seater had been completed and an intensive test and development programme started, culminating in the launch of the XK150's successor in March 1961. Although development of a fixed-head coupe version had been started much later in the programme than the open two-seater, the two cars which were taken to Switzerland, where they became the sensation of the Geneva Salon in much the way as the

original XK120 had taken Earls Court by storm 12 years earlier, were coupes, and with good reason, for they were instantly praised as the most elegant production cars the world had ever been offered. The Jaguar E-type, or XK-E as it was always to be referred to in the United States, had begun a success story which was destined to last for 14 years.

First came that delectable fixed-head coupe and the equally attractive open two-seater, both powered by the 3.8-litre XK engine. There had also been a competition version – a lightweight model based on the open two-seater but with a hardtop permanently in place – of which a dozen examples were built during 1963. These were campaigned by independent entrants, though with discreet factory backing, and they distinguished themselves in international and national GT racing for two seasons.

In October 1964 came the first series of cars with the larger-bore 4.2-litre XK power unit, to be followed in 1966 by a longer-

Its successor was already on its way, and the first public hint of what it would be like came in 1960 when this E-type prototype E2A appeared at Le Mans in Briggs Cunningham's hands.

The definitive E-type roadster as it appeared in 1961 to public acclaim, and the rare competition derivative, the Lightweight E-type, which followed in 1963 and was one of just 12 to be built.

wheelbase 2+2 version of the fixed-head coupe, which was a brave, if aesthetically imperfect attempt to answer criticisms of the lack of cabin space in the existing models. Then came a short period from December 1967 when all three versions were given exposed headlamps and a few minor cosmetic changes which earned them the unofficial appellation Series 1½ until the true Series 2 version arrived in October 1968. These were distinguished by a larger air intake, relocated sidelights and, in the case of the 2+2, a more sloping windscreen to soften this model's side profile in the upper area.

By the time the last of the Series 2 models had left the production line in September 1970, the total of XK-engined E-types had passed the 57,000 mark, of which nearly 42,000 had been 4.2-litre models. But the E-type story was not yet over because, for the second time in Jaguar history, a new engine was ready to be tested in a sports car before it was slipped into the saloon model for which it had primarily been developed.

The 5.3-litre V12 engine was a tight fit in the front of an E-type, which in Series 3 form was made available in just two body styles, coupe and open roadster, both with the 9in longer wheelbase and the more raked windscreen angle previously reserved for the 2+2 model, and with an optional hardtop offered with the open version. The principal distinguishing features of the new line were the front-end panelling and the much deeper air intake, which for the first time carried a grille. With such a heavy engine up front, the latest E-type inevitably lacked the agility of the XK-engined models, but in any case, the basic design was fast approaching its sell-by date, and it came as no surprise when production of the 2+2 coupe version was halted in September 1973, although the last of the open two-seaters was not made until September 1974, by which time over 15,000 Series 3 models had been added to the E-type total.

The biggest surprise was the car which would take its place.

The E-type roadster in its final Series 3 form, with V12 engine and longer-wheelbase bodywork, brought the line to an end in February 1975. The XK story was over, at least for the next 20 or so years.

CHAPTER 2

A NEW DIRECTION

XJS: A late-starting success story

A great deal had happened to Jaguar since 1961, when the original XK series of cars gave way to the XK-engined E-type, and by no means all of it had been for the better. Sir William Lyons (who had been knighted in 1956 for services to export), had outlasted most of his contemporaries as an independent in the British motor industry, but the escalating costs of new product development had been taking their toll, and in order – as he hoped – to safeguard the long-term future of his company following his retirement (he had already passed his 65th birthday) he engaged in a dialogue with BMC, the manufacturers of Austin, Morris, MG, Riley and Wolseley cars, which led in 1966 to a merger. It resulted in the creation of a new umbrella organization, British Motor Holdings (BMH) which, two years down the line, would itself be merged with Standard-Triumph to become the British Leyland Motor Corporation (BLMC, later shortened to BL).

But it all turned out to be a disaster, especially for Jaguar, who continued to haemorrhage financially, became dogged by quality problems, suffered structurally from a period of management centralization following the various mergers, and then had to wait until 1980 to secure once again its independence, and with it the opportunity, under the dynamic leadership of Sir John Egan, to restore both internal morale and customer confidence and lay the foundation for a return to profitability and ultimately to a secure future under new Ford ownership.

On the product side, one of the casualties had been the XJ13 mid-engined sports-racer for which Malcolm Sayer had been given the development go-ahead in 1965 when a possible return of Jaguar to the race tracks had been under consideration. But the funds simply were not available, and to the disappointment of the many thousands of Jaguar racing fans, such a return was still to be many years away. Also short-lived was the possibility of adopting the mid-engined concept for a new Jaguar production sports car; the cost of engineering what would have been a complex car simply did not stand up, nor was it likely to be easy to meet the increasingly stringent safety legislation requirements. A more likely project for acceptance was another of Sayers' concepts for an E-type replacement, which he drew in 1968 in both open and closed coupe forms under the project code XJ21, but this, too, was destined to be stillborn.

End of the line for the traditional Jaguar sports car

Instead, it was decided that the E-type would have to be the end of the line for the traditional Jaguar sports car, at least for the foreseeable future. The new priority was to be the development of a GT model, which

There was a luke-warm reception for the original XJ-S, mainly because such a different replacement for the E-type had been expected.

This was the angle from which the shape of the XJ-S was to prove the most controversial.

hopefully would still appeal to a significant percentage of existing Jaguar sports car customers (many of whom in any case had been calling increasingly vociferously for a more roomy and comfortable driving environment), but the car would also be aimed at a wider market. In particular, the marketing department wished to target the more affluent but still relatively young and performance-conscious business owner or professional, for whom the E-type had been a touch too impractical.

But perhaps most important of all – at least financially – the new model would have to make the maximum possible use of the under-structure and the mechanical componentry of the XJ passenger car range, which had been introduced in 1968. The XJ series had been widely acclaimed, offering new standards of performance, comfort, refinement and quietness, with the help of well-insulated,   subframe-mounted independent suspension all round, so it was a good starting point for what was intended to be a highly refined high-performance coupe.

The first running prototype of the GT derivative, coded XJ27, was produced in 1969, with a wheelbase of 102in – 6in shorter than for the saloon (sedan), but retaining

effectively the same suspension and running gear, but a long gestation period was to follow during which Jaguar's sports car customers became increasing impatient for

XJ-S unveiling provokes a roar of silence

what they assumed would become the 'F-type – son of E-type', a model more or less identical in concept but with the benefit of up-to-the-minute technology. Consequently, the stunned silence which greeted the unveiling of the XJ-S (for Special rather than Sports) in 1975 was due as much to the fact that a fundamentally different car had been expected (despite the factory's attempt to steer the rumour-mongers away from 'F-type' conjecture) as to the new car's comparative lack of traditional Jaguar

23

elegance. There was no question that it was roomier than the E-type, and probably more comfortable, but it was no replacement in the truest sense. But that was the point – it was never intended to be.

Undoubtedly its most controversial feature proved to be the pair of flying buttresses flanking the rear screen, or to be more accurate their unhappy relationship with the outline of the rear side windows aft of the doors. This clash of curves was not in the Jaguar tradition. But the buttresses had been strongly advocated by Malcolm Sayer, who tragically had died in 1970 at the early age of 53, but whose concept of the XJ-S had been left largely unchanged by his successors. Despite his reputation as an inspired one, Sayer had always insisted that he was *not* a stylist, and that the lines he had adopted for his cars had been drawn first and foremost because they were functionally the most efficient. It was the same with his buttresses, the subtle twist of which performed an important aerodynamic function and aided the car's high-speed stability.

All of this, of course, cut little ice with those who had hoped for such a different car, yet the XJ-S (or XJS without the hyphen as it was to be known from 1991) was ultimately to prove a worthy tribute to one of Jaguar's most distinguished employees. Who would have thought that the car which had received such a cool reception on its debut would have a production life of 20 years, during which over 112,000 examples would be produced, also that it would enjoy a distinguished competition career on both sides of the Atlantic?

Sublimely smooth but with a huge thirst for fuel

But the XJ-S was to find the going tough at first. It had only been offered with the 5.3-litre V12 engine, the 285bhp of which gave it a sublimely smooth performance up to a top speed approaching 150mph, but with a horrendous thirst for fuel. This might not have mattered had there not been the

Proving that the early XJ-S was no sports car in the dynamic sense, although there was no disputing the power from its silky V12 engine.

But like a good wine, the XJ-S improved with age, the first important step being the introduction of the HE version with Michael May cylinder heads, which considerably improved fuel consumption and was accompanied by both interior and exterior cosmetic changes.

dreaded Suez Crisis in 1978, which not only restricted oil supplies but caused the price of fuel to rocket. This, and the fact that Jaguar's reliability problems were as yet far from overcome, caused a steady fall in demand, and a reduction in production from almost 3,900 cars in 1977 to 2,400 in 1979 and only just over 1,000 in 1980, by which point serious thought had been given to dropping the 12-cylinder car altogether.

But the arrival in 1981 of the HE (High Efficiency) version of the engine, incorporating high-compression cylinder heads with 'fireball' combustion chambers developed by the Swiss engineer Michael May, saved the day for the V12, improving fuel consumption by well over 20 per cent. The HE models also featured some much-needed upgrading of the cars' interior as well as more attractive five-spoke alloy wheels and

Having offered a targa-topped XK SC as a temporary expedient for fresh-air fans, Jaguar went the whole hog with a full Convertible in 1988, and thereafter it comprehensively outsold the Coupe through to the end of production in 1995.

The Jaguar 6-litre V12 engine was a masterpiece of engineering, but in an ever more environmentally conscious world its long-term potential was always in doubt.

The smoothness of Jaguar's AJ16 4-litre straight-6 engine made it a popular alternative for XJS customers.

other relatively minor but nevertheless important cosmetic improvements. However, it was the restoration of a six-cylinder engine into the sporting Jaguar range in 1983 – not the famous XK this time, but a new-generation AJ6 twin-overhead-camshaft, 24-valve unit – which ensured the long-term future of the XK-S range.

Initially produced in 3.6-litre form, in which it had a maximum output of 225bhp, it was accompanied on its introduction in 1983 by an alternative body, a Cabriolet model with a removable targa-type top, the threatened ban on open cars in the important US market having long since been proved ill-founded. The XJ-SC became a popular model, demand invariably outstripping supply, but it was relatively short-lived, being replaced by a full Convertible in 1985.

It was during the Eighties that Jaguar, in partnership with Tom Walkinshaw's TWR Group, returned victoriously to Le Mans and the World Sportscar Championship scene, taking the Championship in 1987 and the Le Mans race in 1988 with purpose-built TWR-constructed Jaguar XKR-9 cars. In order to exploit these track successes, Jaguar and Walkinshaw established JaguarSport, a joint-venture company, to build and offer for sale higher-performance versions of Jaguar's mainstream production cars. The first product of the new company was the XJR-S, based on the 5.3-litre V12 XJ-S, with uprated suspension, 15-inch Speedline wheels with Pirelli P600 235/60VR-15 tyres and modified steering. Other visual changes were body-coloured front and rear bumpers, sill mouldings and a rear spoiler, plus a black satin finish to the radiator grille and headlamp bezels. The first 100 cars, classified

Capitalizing on the XJ-S's success in the European Touring Car Championship, this XJR-S version was launched in 1988 and was produced in limited quantities by JaguarSport, an offshoot company at the time jointly owned by Jaguar and TWR, who were masterminding Jaguar's successful return to endurance racing.

as 'Celebration' models, were finished in Tungsten Grey metallic paint with matching Doeskin leather upholstery with Savile Grey piping and stitching.

The next major milestone came in 1991 with the only major body change in the GT Jaguar's 20-year production story. Most people, hearing that it was imminent, had assumed that the flying buttresses would finally disappear, but once again they were to be proved wrong, the main change in that area being to the side windows, which gave the XJS Coupe a harmony of line which hitherto had been lacking. Both the front and the rear of the cars were restyled around the bumper and lights area, and there was a further major revamp of the interior, especially the dashboard, where the earlier barrel-type minor instruments, which had never been popular, gave way to conventional circular dials in a completely remodelled facia. The main change mechanically was the replacement of the 3.6-litre six-cylinder engine with a longer-stroke 4-litre version, which offered a similar maximum output to the earlier engine despite the addition of the now mandatory catalyst. Along with the venerable V12, the new six-cylinder would

28

The buttresses survived the long-awaited restyling of the XJS body, proving that it was the clash with the rear side window profile which had been the aesthetic problem. The revised glassware did the trick.

see the XJS range through to the end of production in 1995.

Ford ownership leads to major leap in quality

But the most important change from 1991 onwards was not instantly visible, yet it was perhaps the most important change of all. In 1989 the Ford Motor Company had bought Jaguar Cars for what at the time seemed to be an excessively large sum of money, especially when a close inspection by the American company's top executives revealed that they had inherited some fairly antiquated production facilities. It was the lack of finance to rip out and replace these which had been behind so many of Jaguar's quality problems, but Ford management was prepared, in fact had no option, but to take the long-term view, and they instantly committed further major funds to completely change Jaguar's production facilities, procedures and components sourcing.

The results were quickly apparent in a spectacular upturn in product quality and reliability, which was an essential requirement in restoring the international prestige of the marque. It was therefore with a feeling of great confidence that the company's engineering staff were able to turn themselves to the enviable task of developing an entirely new range of sports models. However, in doing so it was important that they looked back as well as forward, to identify and remember the major strengths which had been demonstrated in their heyday, first by the XKs and then by the E-types, as well as the strengths of the XJS models which, after surviving such a difficult beginning, had matured into desirable GT models for which sales had been sustained beyond all reasonable expectations.

CHAPTER 3

BACK TO A SPORTS CAR

Project X100

At the time of Ford's purchase of Jaguar Cars, a project already in a fairly advanced stage of development, coded XJ41, was for a 2+2 shorter-chassis spin-off, in closed coupe form only, from the XJ40 series of saloons (sedans) which had been introduced in 1986. Never a top priority for Jaguar during what had been a difficult time for the company, XK41 had been around for several years, and during that time it had grown in size, in weight, in complexity and inevitably in cost. Substantial additional funding would now be necessary to carry the project through to production, but even if this could have been found – which was far from likely in view of the many other calls by Jaguar on Ford's financial resources at that time – XJ41, far from being a worthy successor to XJS, smacked of being simply too much more of the same sort of thing. So the new management lost little time in halting the programme, and the considerable sum which had already been invested in it was effectively written-off, at least so far as Jaguar was concerned, although in further developed form it was to have a second life as the basis for the Aston Martin DB7.

Notwithstanding the commercial success of the XJS, its very existence had opened a significant gap in the product range for something very different – because Jaguar no longer had a true sports car, for which potential customers were becoming increasingly impatient. With adequate rescources available to the company for the first time – always provided the financial justification for any proposal was able to survive the notoriously tough scrutiny routinely applied by Ford's top management – there was every hope that this gap could finally be filled.

It was deemed essential, most particularly by those whose memories went back to the launch of the original XJ-S in 1975, that any such new model, in addition to having all the necessary performance attributes, would have to simply ooze style. Memories of the original XK120 and the Series 1 E-type, and the rapturous receptions which they had received at their launch, were still talked about with a mixture of pride and sadness in the corridors at Browns Lane, for nothing quite like it had been seen since.

Style the priority as design teams are set to work

So this time style had to be a priority, in fact such was its importance that the company's stylists were encouraged to make almost uninhibited use of the paint brush and sketch pad, and to be as bold as they dared. Inevitably, they were encouraged to borrow cues from past models or discarded ideas, because what was needed at the end of the day was not just a stylish car, but a stylish Jaguar – a car whose shape would

The X100 project team were encouraged to remember successful styling ideas from the past, even though they may not have been on cars which actually went into production. This 1979 exercise by Pininfarina, whose XJ Spider was based on the XJS, was clearly one of the inspirations for the new car's nose treatment.

Imitation is the best form of flattery, and there were echoes of the Pininfarina car in the nose of the XJ220 supercar, which a team of enthusiastic employees under the leadership of Jaguar's former design chief Jim Randall produced in their spare time in 1988 and which ultimately went into limited production four years later.

immediately point to its birthplace. There was certainly an abundance of material from which to 'poach' attractive features, ranging from the Pininfarina-styled and XJS-based Spyder which had been exhibited as a consumer-response exercise at the 1978 British Motor Show at the NEC, near Birmingham, to the fabulous but ill-fated limited-edition XJ220 supercar, which had recently been revealed and was to be produced by JaguarSport Ltd – the offshoot company then still jointly owned by Jaguar Cars and Tom Walkinshaw's TWR Group – in response to what initially had seemed a huge demand, only for it to evaporate almost overnight when another Suez Crisis marked the death-knell of the breed.

Teams from the UK, USA and Italy in styling contest

The different styling teams – which included an input from Ford's own styling centres both in Dearborn, USA and at the former Ghia premises in Turin, Italy – were

This was Clay 1, Ghia of Turin's suggestion for a traditional form of luxury GT car. It was not adopted, but the oval grille was remembered when the time came to style Jaguar's S-class.

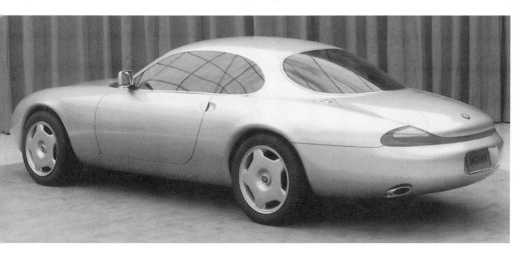

Clay 2 was a more radical approach, although some of its excesses had been toned down by the time it appeared in this form, to survive as a candidate at a third styling review.

charged with the task of considering one of four different approaches, which were identified as being evolutionary, evocative, progressive and radical; their best efforts would then be taken through to the clay mock-up stage for a series of presentation clinics to be held at intervals during 1992. All had to use the XJS floorpan as the foundation of their respective proposals, which were to be for a closed coupe, although it was envisaged that an open version would also be offered when the chosen car was eventually put into production.

The first approach, which was tackled by the Ghia team, was in deference to Jaguar's existing customer base, the people who were currently running an XJS; the second, which was handled by the Jaguar studio at Whitley, was an attempt to recapture something of the spirit and substance of the E-type; the third, which became the responsibility of the Dearborn centre, concentrated more on currently fashionable ideas; while the fourth, also a Whitley creation, ignored Jaguar tradition and went instead for radical new shapes.

The first to fall by the wayside was the progressive approach, the clay of which was considered to be insufficiently different from the XJS in concept, and it was followed later by the traditional and radical proposals, neither of which, though worthy in themselves, had sufficient 'Jaguar' in their styling theme. This left the evocative proposal from the Whitley team, which was felt to be closest to the target, though it had yet to score a bull's-eye. It was certainly an elegant shape, to which alternative air intakes, lighting arrangements and other cosmetic appendages were applied at different times, but it was still not quite right; specifically, it looked too large, and it was felt that it would appear better balanced if there was a little less overhang at the front and considerably less bodywork behind the rear wheels.

Accordingly, a further clay was produced, which was to be used for another clinic where it would be presented as an alternative alongside the earlier proposal, this in turn having also undergone minor changes in the interim. By this stage each of the clays had been given a variation on the open-style elliptical air intake which, doubtless inspired by the D-type, XJ220 and others, would eventually feature on the production version. The 'contest' was a close-run thing, but ultimately the nod was given to the newer clay, which featured a larger but lower-positioned intake and the layout of head and

A progressive theme was entrusted to Ford's stylists in Dearborn and this Clay 3 was the result, being offered here in two versions with a centreline split. Like Ghia's offering, it was not selected.

auxiliary lights which was to become such a distinguishing feature of the XK8.

Meanwhile, the painstaking efforts to

Designers play with five ways to trim a cat

develop precisely the right exterior style were matched by the care with which the different proposals for the interior, and in particular

the dashboard area and centre console, were created and evaluated. In this instance five different approaches were considered, these being identified as traditional, progressive, evolutionary, avant-garde and radical. The first was to be derived from saloon (sedan) treatments already in production or in preparation; the second involved using a central spine as the dominant feature of the facia; the third featured woodwork across the full width of the dashboard and along the door tops; the fourth was a mass of curving lines with an absence of woodwork; and the fifth, perhaps appropriately, was even more radical, with an offset curving panel extending three-quarters of the way across the facia.

Although a great deal of effort had gone into creating these very different proposals, the task of selecting one of them was a lot

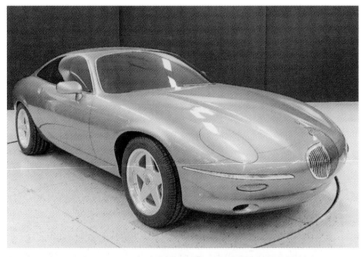

Clay 4, by the Jaguar team at Whitley, was considered the best of the quartet and was chosen to be taken forward to the refinement stages, which would involve the production of two more clays, coded A and M.

Getting closer to the final product, Clay M finally emerged in this form (above) when it was presented at a clinic as an alternative to Clay A (below).

Clay A initially suffered from too heavy a tail treatment, but this was lightened by an upswept wing line with the lower panel in a contrasting colour.

Late in the day Clays M and A were combined for presentation in convertible form, from which Clay A, with its lower and larger air intake and characteristic headlamp treatment, was finally chosen.

easier than for the car's exterior, for the progressive effort was judged to be the only one suitable for serious consideration. However, it was a long way from being acceptable, so once again a further proposal was called for to be judged against it. It emerged as a very different design, featuring a full-width wood-faced panel with a broad centre console below and separate from it. It was by far the more attractive layout, so it went forward for modelling and was duly chosen to accompany the selected exterior in October 1992.

At this stage, however, the car which would carry the XK8 name was still far from a certainty, for the funding for the full X100 programme had yet to be secured. In fact, Jaguar's financial performance at that time was so parlous that there was a real possibility that the whole programme would have to be canned. Although preparations for the out-sourcing of components had

Suppliers keep faith as Jaguar strives for Ford funding

proceeded, these had only been possible thanks to the faith and goodwill of the potential suppliers, and there followed an

This glassfibre model, produced as a display car in 1992, was the first indication of the final form in which the production XK8 Coupe would eventually appear.

Two alternative treatments were considered once the decision had been taken to go for a full-width dashboard with a 'Spitfire wing' profile and a separate centre console.

agonizing year during which Jaguar management, led by project leader Bob Dover (who was later to be appointed chief executive of Aston Martin, and subsequent to that of Land Rover when it, too, came under Ford ownership), worked tirelessly to take cost out of the programme without jeopardizing the quality and integrity of the end product. It was a desperately difficult task, but it was handled brilliantly, so much so that Ford finally gave the programme the go-ahead in December 1993.

The euphoria throughout the factory when this news broke was total, but there was precious little time for celebrations by the X100 project team, who now had to advance the programme through the many prototype construction and quality and endurance testing stages before it could be signed off for production. The schedule was desperately tight, because the XK8 was due to make its show debut at Geneva in March 1996, to be followed soon afterwards by a presentation in New York, and the car had to be in production by the time of the British motor show the following October.

During 1993 such component development as had taken place had involved the use of simulators, mostly XJS coupes and convertibles modified as necessary to accept the new V8 engine, driveline, suspensions and/or inner structure intended for the XK8. This had also enabled useful work to be carried out on crash testing and on the performance evaluation of engine management systems. But once X100 had been given the green light, it was time to rush through a whole fleet of mechanical prototypes, of which more than 50 would be constructed and in use by the summer of 1994, half of them still clothed in XJS bodywork because they would be performing

The first real indication of what the production Convertible would look like was provided by this prototype produced in 1993, again in glassfibre, for display purposes. The two versions of the XK8 were to be announced simultaneously in 1996.

their duties largely outside the factory. Much of the cold-weather testing, for example, was to take place in Canada, while other prototypes were taken to Arizona for endurance running in extreme heat. Meanwhile, some of the first prototypes clothed in X100 bodywork were used for a further programme of crash tests under cover.

By the end of the year much of the preliminary work had been completed and it became the turn of a new series of evaluation prototypes to be used to fine-tune everything from engine management and cooling systems to air conditioning performance, braking efficiency, body sealing, levels of noise, vibration and harshness, as well as to carry out more of the seemingly interminable crash testing. Nearly 30 additional prototypes were built for this work during the winter of 1994/95, the bodywork being split almost evenly between Coupes and Convertibles. They were kept busy through much of 1995 before the

Most of the mechanical prototypes were camouflaged as XJS models, but beneath the familiar skin were the new car's front and rear suspensions, the 4-litre V8 engine and its automatic transmission.

Many thousands of miles were covered on test tracks and in remote regions in extremes of climate before the X100 project could be passed off for production.

The surrounding crate is lifted, and the XK8 Coupe is revealed to the Press in Geneva. The car's reception echoed that which the E-type had received at the same event 35 years earlier.

43

From the start of production the XK8's cockpit was to be offered in two finishes, this being the Sport interior, featuring a maple veneer covering for the dashboard, a fully leather-covered steering wheel and gear knob and a dark facia surround.

The alternative Classic interior offered burr walnut on the dashboard, a part-wood, part-leather steering wheel and matching wood gear knob. In both cases the three central dials would be replaced by digitial readouts when their space was required for a navigation screen.

programme moved into its final phase that autumn with the construction of the first of the verification prototypes, the vehicles which would finally confirm the detailed production specification of the XK8. Over 30 of these cars were to be constructed, again split almost evenly between Coupes and Convertibles, and the last example of each of them, built in January 1996, was to be used as the show car at Geneva and New York, respectively.

When the wraps came off that gleaming blue Coupe on the Jaguar stand in Geneva it was the final act of a programme which had occupied Bob Dover and his project team for some six years and had involved an up-front expenditure of many millions of pounds and dollars. For those members of the task force who were present in Switzerland that day, therefore, the unveiling of the XK8 was a tense moment, but they need not have worried because the audience reaction was just what was needed; they simply loved it. Those painful memories of the relative silence with which the original XJ-S had been greeted in 1975 had finally been laid to rest.

Bob Dover, subsequently Jaguar's manufacturing director, then boss of Aston Martin and most recently of Land Rover, was the project leader of the X100 team.

Project approval for X100 was a time for brief celebration and a photocall. Here, Bob Dover is leaning on the car roof, surrounded by 17 of his 22 colleagues who helped to bring the XK8 into being.

The Convertible in this picture is displaying the standard 17in wheels with which the car was introduced, while the Coupe has the optional seven-spoke 18in alloys.

The XK8 Coupe is an attractive looking car from every angle, but in side profile it has to be one of the most beautiful shapes ever to grace a production car.

The constant rise of Jaguar engine efficiency

The following table offers a comparison of maximum power outputs of Jaguar sports models and their engines from the XK120 to the XKR.

XK120	3,442cc	160bhp @ 5,000rpm	46.48bhp/litre (SAE)
XK140	3,442cc	190bhp @ 5,500rpm	55.20bhp/litre (SAE)
XK150S	3,442cc	250bhp @ 5,500rpm	72.63bhp/litre (SAE)
XK150S	3,781cc	265bhp @ 5,500rpm	70.08bhp/litre (SAE)
E-type S1	3,781cc	265bhp @ 5,500rpm	70.08bhp/litre (SAE)
E-type S3	5,343cc	272bhp @ 5,850rpm	50.90bhp/litre (DIN)
XJ-S	5,343cc	285bhp @ 5,500rpm	53.34bhp/litre (DIN)
XJ-S HE	5,343cc	295bhp @ 5,000rpm	55.21bhp/litre (DIN)
XJR-S	5,343cc	318bhp @ 5,000rpm	59.51bhp/litre (DIN)
XJ-S 3.6	3,590cc	225bhp @ 5,300rpm	62.67bhp/litre (DIN)
XJS	5,994cc	308bhp @ 5,350rpm	51.38bhp/litre (DIN)
XJS 4.0	3,980cc	223bhp @ 4,750rpm	56.03bhp/litre (DIN)
XJR-S	5,994cc	318bhp @ 5,250rpm	53.05bhp/litre (DIN)
XK8	3,995cc	290bhp @ 6,100rpm	72.59bhp/litre (DIN)
XKR	3,995cc	370bhp @ 6,150rpm	92.61bhp/litre (DIN)

A comparison of maximum torque figures of Jaguar sports models and their engines.

XK120	3,442cc	195lb.ft @ 2,500rpm	56.65lb.ft/litre (SAE)
XK140	3,442cc	210lb.ft @ 2,500rpm	61.01lb.ft/litre (SAE)
XK150S	3,442cc	240lb.ft @ 4,500rpm	69.72lb.ft/litre (SAE)
XK150S	3,781cc	260lb.ft @ 4,000rpm	68.76lb.ft/litre (SAE)
E-type S1	3,781cc	260lb.ft @ 4,000rpm	68.76lb.ft/litre (SAE)
E-type S3	5,343cc	304lb.ft @ 3,600rpm	56.89lb.ft/litre (DIN)
XJ-S	5,343cc	294lb.ft @ 3,500rpm	55.02lb.ft/litre (DIN)
XJ-S HE	5,343cc	318lb.ft @ 3,500rpm	59.51lb.ft/litre (DIN)
XJR-S	5,343cc	348lb.ft @ 3,650rpm	65.13lb.ft/litre (DIN)
XJ-S 3.6	3,590cc	240lb.ft @ 4,000rpm	66.85lb.ft/litre (DIN)
XJS	5,994cc	355lb.ft @ 2,850rpm	59.22lb.ft/litre (DIN)
XJS 4.0	3,980cc	278lb.ft @ 3,650rpm	69.84lb.ft/litre (DIN)
XJR-S	5,994cc	365lb.ft @ 3,650rpm	60.89lb.ft/litre (DIN)
XK8	3,995cc	290lb.ft @ 4,250rpm	72.59lb.ft/litre (DIN)
XKR	3,995cc	387lb.ft @ 3,600rpm	96.87lb.ft/litre (DIN)

The Jaguar AJ-V8 engine on display – a masterpiece of compact packaging as well as of operational efficiency.

CHAPTER 4

THE XK8 IN DETAIL – 1

Engine and transmission

Although it is generally agreed that the heart of a new car is its engine, within the motor industry there is a widely held belief that a new car and a new engine should never be introduced simultaneously. The cost accountants will argue for phased introductions on the grounds that they spread what could otherwise be an intolerable financial burden in having to fund the development and launch of both car and engine at the same time. They are also likely to have the support of their marketing colleagues, who will always welcome the opportunity to 're-launch' an existing model with a new engine.

Certainly, Jaguar's engine history has tended to follow this route of phased introductions. Although the company's first truly in-house engine, the famous 3.4-litre XK, was initially revealed in the brand new XK120 roadster, this car, as explained earlier, was intended to be merely a temporary, limited-production gap-filling exercise pending the introduction of the engine's true 'home', the Mk VII. The second engine, the 5.3-litre V12, was used in 1971 to freshen-up the E-type's image after the car had been in production for a decade, while the third engine, the 3.6-litre AJ6 of 1983, was similarly used to broaden the market of the XJ-S after the V12 version had already been around for eight years.

But the engineers entrusted with the design and development of what was to become the XK8 had set themselves some formidable targets: to deliver the highest possible standards of performance per litre, performance per pound weight, refinement,

fuel efficiency and emissions cleanliness from the engine, in unison with the equally exacting standards set for the car's handling, ride, roadholding, steering response and braking efficency, as well as very high levels of luxury, comfort and quietness for the occupants. These standards, which in some cases conflicted, could, they felt, best be achieved if X100, as it was then known, was designed, developed and ultimately introduced as a complete package.

Choices of engine configuration and component packaging

Although in the interim other elements of the car could be tackled in isolation, it was not until the engine configuration had been settled and its dimensions and weight estimated with a considerable degree of accuracy that the proposed car could begin to be considered as a complete entity. Conversely, the packaging of surrounding components and equipment, including the front suspension, steering, transmission and the ever increasing amount of engine-associated ancillary material demanded of a 21st Century high-performance luxury car needed also to be considered in assessing the

The multi-layered aluminium alloy castings of the AJ-V8 on view with the crankshaft sandwiched between the structural bed plate and the upper block casting.

The V8 engine's lubrication system showing the feeds to the crankshaft bearings, camshafts and timing chain tensioners.

relative value of the various engine options which were available.

These embraced everything from six to 12 cylinders, although the 'six' was quickly discarded as being unlikely to meet the performance targets if it was also to offer the required levels of refinement and emissions control. The V10 option was also dismissed because of its inherent lack of balance, while a V12 was considered to be too bulky, too heavy and too thirsty. Hence the decision to design what would become Jaguar's first production V8 engine. Internally it was first given the codename XJ26 (a progression from the AJ6 six-cylinder engine and its derivative AJ16), but when various revisions were introduced during the 1999 model-year,

as detailed in Chapter 7, the code became AJ27. However, prior to the engine's launch in its original form the designation was to be changed in the public domain to the more logical and descriptive AJ-V8. Such is the importance of Jaguar's latest production engine, which undoubtedly in the course of time will also power a variety of yet-to-be-announced cars from the same stable, that a detailed look at its components and features – and those of its transmission as fitted to the XK8 – is now appropriate.

A displacement of at least 4 litres was deemed necessary to meet the performance targets, and after both longer-stroke and shorter-stroke alternatives had also been considered ‘– the former involving work with

Although a five-valve layout was considered, combining three inlets and two exhausts, a four-valve combustion chamber was preferred because of the larger inlet valve diameter this allowed.

the combination of an 83mm bore and 92mm stroke – the decision was taken to 'go square' with both the cylinder bore and the stroke set at 86mm to give a displacement of 3,996cc. Although it took barely a year from conception for the first V8 engine to be

Four years of development and 200 prototypes

completed, this was the first of more than 200 prototypes of various types to be produced during a development cycle which lasted some four years before the final production specification was passed off in every detail.

The structure of the AJ-V8 production engine comprises a multi-layered assembly of aluminium alloy castings, two of which are united to form the cylinder block. The upper part of the block, which supplies the platforms onto which the two cylinder heads are mounted, is a die-casting which sits on top of a separate structural bedplate casting incorporating the main bearing caps and featuring a cast iron insert in each of the main bearing positions. A further aluminium casting provides the upper part of the sump, into which the oil filter mounting and oil cooler diverter valve assembly and ports are cast, and the sump is closed by a pressed-steel oil pan. A windage tray attached to the top of the structural body isolates the oil pan from the air disturbed by the rotation of the crankshaft in order to prevent oil aeration and to improve drainage. The rear of the sump, the bedplate and the cylinder block are heavily braced into the transmission bellhousing to provide an exceptionally stiff power train.

The five-bearing crankshaft, which carries six balance weights, is made of spheroidal graphite cast iron and operates the short-skirt, flat-top, three-ringed, aluminium pistons through forged connecting rods. In place of conventional iron liners, the cylinder bores in the upper block casting are Nikasil-coated by piston supplier Mahle – a plating process which offers the advantages of weight saving as well as providing a smooth rubbing surface to minimize both piston friction and oil consumption.

The two cylinder heads – which are produced by Cosworth's low-pressure sand-casting process – carry four 28mm diameter, internally drilled cast iron camshafts, the inlets being chain-driven from the crankshaft and in turn driving the exhaust cams through a further pair of short chains. One of the reasons why chain drive was chosen in preference to belt drive was because it was possible with the dual-chain drive to accommodate one of the chains within the 18mm offset of the two cylinder banks,

thereby enabling a shorter engine to be produced than would have been possible had a wider belt drive been chosen. But perhaps a more important consideration was the perceived greater durability of chains and the need to ensure that in the event of a drive failure, engine damage would be confined to the valve gear.

Each of the four chains is hydraulically tensioned, the same oil being used to provide lubrication through a bleed hole. The tensioner blade on each inlet cam chain pivots at its top to provide optimal control of the chain as it leaves the crankshaft, and on all four chains the tensioner is mounted on the slack side for improved control. The chains for each cylinder bank are set out of phase by half a tooth to reduce noise. All the chain tensioners, blades, guides and dampers are made from a lightweight and durable Polyamide composite material.

The engine-driven accessories – alternator

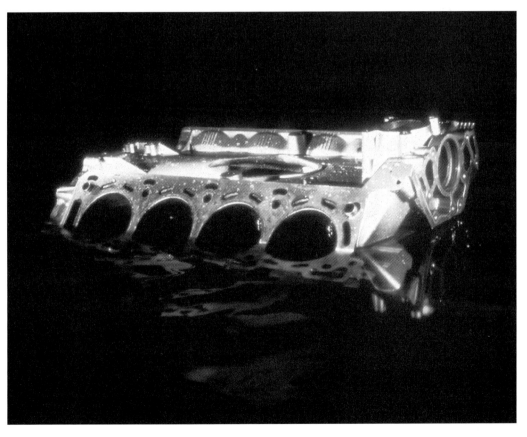

Nikasil electroplating of the cylinder bores does away with the need for iron liners in the aluminium alloy block, thereby reducing friction and weight.

Cooling of the cylinder block is split, half the coolant being diverted direct to the heads before being routed to rejoin the other half and contribute to the cooling of the cylinder bores.

and power steering, water and air conditioner pumps – are all driven by a single seven-rib poly-vee belt from the crankshaft damper, the belt being automatically tensioned by a coil spring and guided by a secondary idler; manufactured from a Tozone material, the belt is claimed to have a service life in excess of 100,000 miles.

The cams operate two lightweight 35mm inlet and 31mm exhaust valves per cylinder, the pairs of valves being set at the narrow included angle of just 28deg. During the development phase, a five-valve layout was also examined, but the larger diameters made possible with the four-valve solution was favoured in the interests of superior high-speed breathing. The inlet camshafts are equipped with VCP, a Variable Cam Phasing system through which the cams are advanced at low speeds to achieve earlier closure so as to increase torque and retarded at high speeds to achieve maximum power by delaying valve closure, the system being controlled by a pair of electronically switched oil presure control valves by means of solenoids linked to the engine's ECM (Electronic Control Module). In a further weight-saving measure the inlet manifold has been moulded in a composite plastic material, into which the fuel rail has been integrated. The eight injectors feed into compact pent roof combustion chambers which, in conjunction with the flat-top pistons, offer a compression ratio of 10.75:1.

The EMS (Engine Management System) was developed by Jaguar in collaboration with the Japanese experts Nippondenso, who set up a laboratory in Coventry for the purpose. In addition to its usual functions of controlling the fuel/air feed and ignition

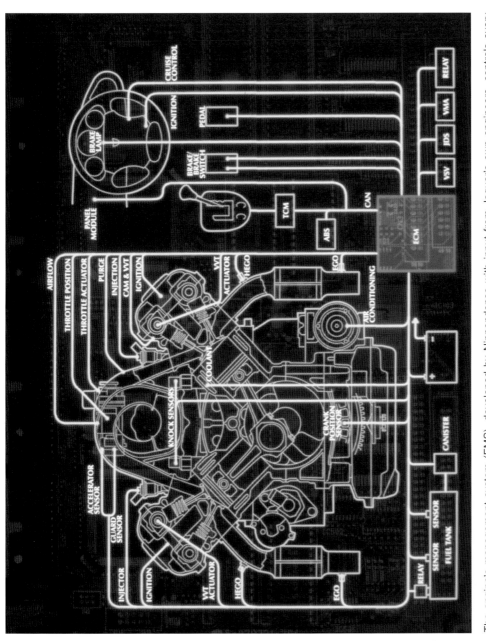

The engine's management system (EMS), developed by Nippondenso with input from Jaguar's own engineers, controls every aspect of engine performance and emissions control through an elaborate system of sensors.

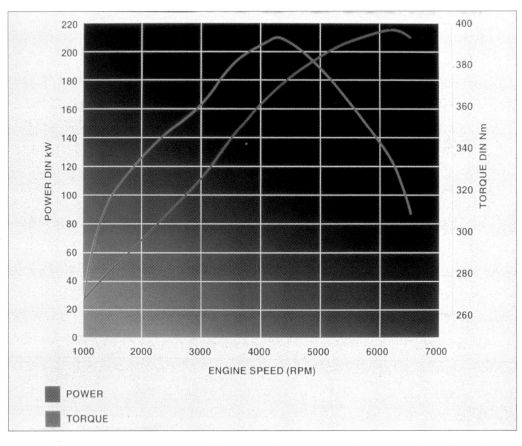

Power and torque curves for the Jaguar AJ-V8 engine, which reveal not only its high-revving ability, with peak power reached at 6,200rpm, but also the flexibility which comes with such a fat torque curve, 300Nm being delivered from as low as 1,500rpm.

timing, in adverse conditions it can also provide an Automatic Stability Control (ASC) function whereby engine power is decreased

Impressive torque obviates need for manual gearbox

electronically to combat wheelspin (like current Formula One cars, the XK8 has a fly-by-wire system with no physical link between engine and accelerator pedal).

The efficiency of the EMS has played a significant role in achieving the XJ-V8

engine's impressive performance figures, which include a maximum output of 290bhp (216kW) at 6,100rpm and maximum torque of 290lb.ft (393Nm) at 4,250rpm, with over 80 per cent of the maximum torque figure being sustained all the way through the rev range from 1,400 to 6,400rpm.

This spectacular torque output was one of the factors which prompted the decision not to offer the XK8 with a manual gearbox, but to concentrate instead on optimizing the performance of a five-speed electronically controlled automatic transmission. Built to a specification laid down by Jaguar's engineers, it was designed and developed by ZF and incorporates the popular J-gate selector through which a considerable degree of manual control can be achieved.

The right-hand side of the selector gate offers the driver the usual 'P R N and D' positions, the last-named offering fully automatic selection of any of the five forward

56

gears, while after moving the lever to the left the driver is given the choice of '4', '3' and '2' for manual selection.

Gearshift points controlled by 32-bit module

The gearshifting points in the automatic mode are selected through electro-hydraulic valves operated by the 32-bit control module, resulting in virtually seemless changes of gear, the Lexus having been taken as the benchmark during the development phase. The control module selects the gearshift points as a function of vehicle speed, engine load and of course selector and mode switch positions, and it also adjusts the shift points for extremes of temperature, traction control, cruise-speed control (to eliminate hunting between gears) and road gradient. When traction control mode is activated a transmission programme is implemented which eliminates unwanted downshifts, thereby reducing wheelspin, while during high g-force cornering gearshifts are inhibited to maintain stability. The transmission incorporates a low-inertia torque converter, and an electronically activated lock-up allows a controlled amount of slip when the higher gears are in use at low road speeds.

The use of five forward ratios has enabled a particularly low first gear of 3.57:1 to be adopted to meet US demands for rapid initial acceleration from rest – the 'stoplight Grand Prix' – at the same time as offering an overdrive fifth of 0.80:1 for relaxed and economical cruising. There is a straight run for the propshaft from the back of the gearbox to the rear differential, which is located on the car's centreline, thereby avoiding the usual angled run necessary to meet an offset pinion. With a final-drive ratio of 3.06:1, the XK8 is travelling at 32mph per 1,000rpm in top gear and at approximately 40mph per 1,000rpm when the overdrive fifth is engaged.

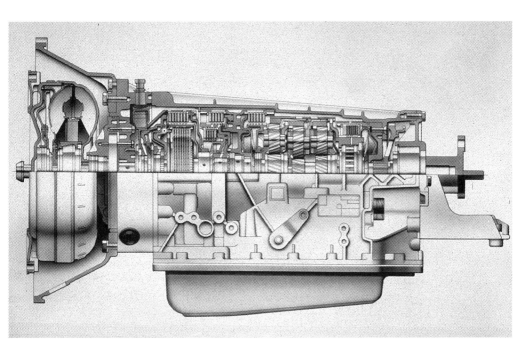

The XK8's ZF 5HP24 five-speed automatic transmission in which gears are shifted electro-hydraulically with the aid of a 32-bit control module.

The famous Jaguar J-gate as applied to the XK8. The two buttons in the foreground are the master switch for the cruise control and the selector for setting the sport or normal driveline mode.

The transmission is a 'fill for life' unit, which precludes the need for a dipstick and the traditional fluid level checks, but as with the AJ-V8 engine, the electronic system incorporates a full on-board diagnostic capability – a Californian requirement – through which any engine or transmission defect will be exposed for rapid analysis and correction. Low maintenance cost has been high on the list of Jaguar's design requirements from the moment that the XK8 was conceived.

CHAPTER 5

THE XK8 IN DETAIL – 2

Structure and running gear

One of the reasons why Jaguars have traditionally been renowned for excellent road noise suppression is that their suspension has not been located directly onto the main underframe, but instead has been mounted on a separate crossbeam which in turn is then attached through insulating bushes to the main structure. Both the XJS and the X300 saloon (sedan) beams were examined for possible adaptation for the XK8, but neither was found to be suitable, mainly because of the different location of the V8 engine and the positioning of its sump towards the front of the unit rather than at the back, as was the case with both the six-cylinder and V12 engines.

So a purpose-built crossbeam was produced, initially in steel for the first prototype tests, but subsequently as an aluminium alloy die-casting, which not only saved more than 7kg in weight, but proved better able to be controlled in manufacture and to pass the exacting fatigue tests. The XK8's front suspension is a double-wishbone system, the upper links being attached to pillars on the end of the crossbeam, while the wider-based lower wishbones are mounted on the underside of the beam. Coaxial coil springs and dampers are mounted direct to the body within the wishbone links and an anti-roll bar is routed forwards around the base of the V8 engine.

As at the front, the rear suspension is mounted on a detachable subframe, thereby helping to insulate the main body structure from road shocks. Again, upper and lower links control the suspension geometry, transverse and trailing arms providing the lower links and the drive-shafts functioning as the upper links. The linkages thus formed provide both anti-squat under acceleration and anti-lift under braking, and coaxial springs and dampers and a rear anti-roll bar complete the suspension package.

Specifications offer four choices of ride and handling

However, XK8 customers are offered a choice of four variations on the car's ride and handling theme. The standard specification involves the fitment of 17in diameter and 8in wide five-spoke cast alloy wheels shod with Pirelli 245/50ZR-17 P Zero tyres, but there is a Sport option with cars supplied on 18in diameter seven-spoke alloy wheels with 245/45ZR-18 P Zero tyres with directional treads at the front and 255/45ZR-18 P Zeros with assymetric treads at the rear. As, of course, these front and rear tyres are not interchangeable, cars fitted with them are supplied with a space-saver 3.5J x 18in spare wheel with a 135/80R-18 tyre. Subtle variations in suspension settings come with the 18in option. But whether the 17in or 18in wheels are preferred, XK8 Coupes are also available optionally with CATS

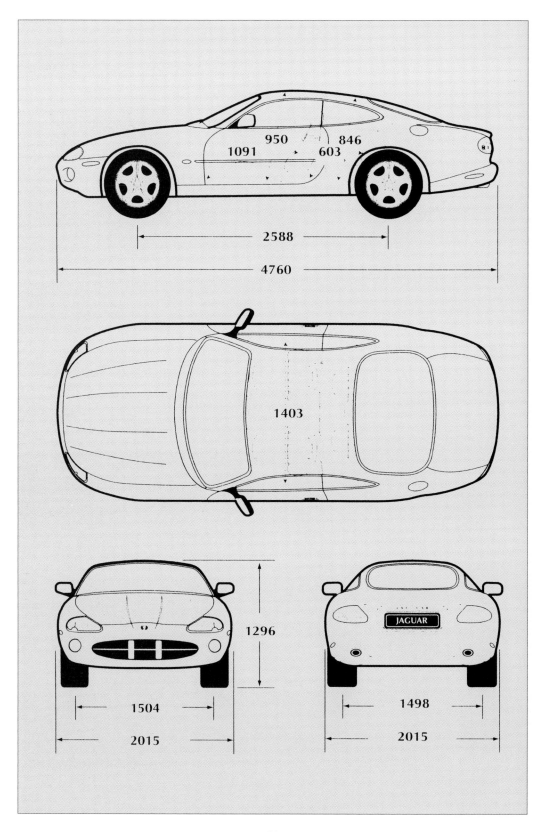

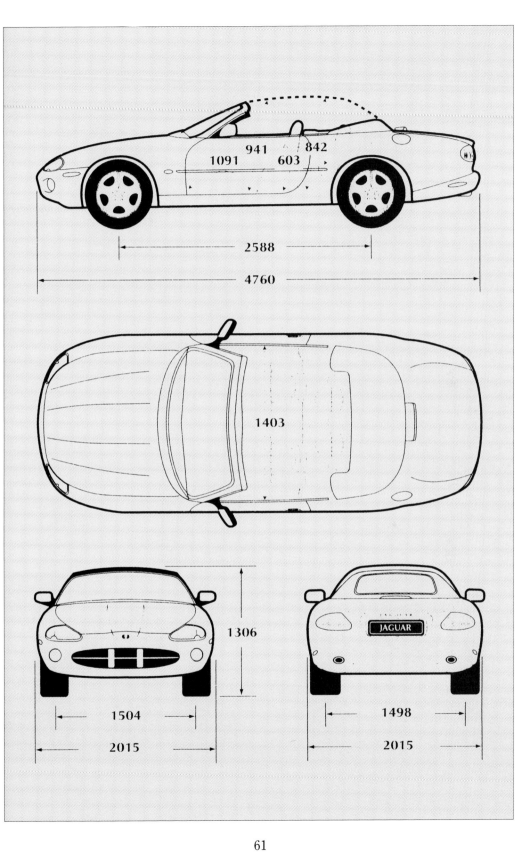

941 842
1091 603

2588

4760

1403

1306

1504

2015

JAGUAR

1498

2015

As installed in the XK8 the AJ-V8 engine evenly straddles the front suspension towers. Jaguar's V8 engines are produced in a purpose-built extension of Ford's impressive Bridgend engine-manufacturing facility in South Wales.

(Computer Active Technlogy Suspension), involving uprated springs and ACD (Active Controlled Dampers), in which an ECU selects the settings most appropriate to the current road and driving conditions.

Variable-ratio rack for optimum low and high-speed steering

The full benefits of a meticulously tailored suspension cannot be enjoyed without equal care having been given to the steering, and the XK8's ZF Servotronic rack-and-pinion system is certainly better than most. Building on the specification developed for the X300 saloons (sedans), in which the amount of power assistance available was varied according to speed, the X100 team added a variable-ratio rack, with the spacing of the rack teeth increasing towards the outer ends of the rack so that both slow-speed manoeuvring (for parking) and emergency high-speed deviations can be assisted without detriment to normal steering responses within a total gearing of just 2.8 turns from full lock to lock. This produces a turning circle of 36ft 2in, which is 6ft 7in more compact than that of the XJS.

Developed in collaboration with Teves, the braking system involves the use of outboard-mounted ventilated discs all round, 305mm in diameter (increased to 325mm at the front during the 1999 model year) and 28mm wide, and a Mk 20 three-channel ABS anti-lock system. It also forms part of the XK8's Traction Control (TC) system which, acting in conjunction with the Automatic Stability Control (ASC), has the ability to apply the two rear-wheel brakes independently, giving an effect similar to a limited-slip differential, this being particularly beneficial during hard acceleration on a slippery surface, especially if the amount of grip available beneath each of the rear wheels differs. In these conditions

Notwithstanding the intrusion of the regulation UK number-plate, the large oval intake allows a plentiful air supply into the Jaguar XK8's engine compartment, even in high ambient temperatures. The jaguar growler on the nose badge peers out of a green background with a black outer ring.

Luggage accommodation in the XK8 Coupe is surprisingly generous by sports car standards, the available space extending well forward of this suspended but detachable net seen here for carrying small items, which was introduced with the year-2000 models.

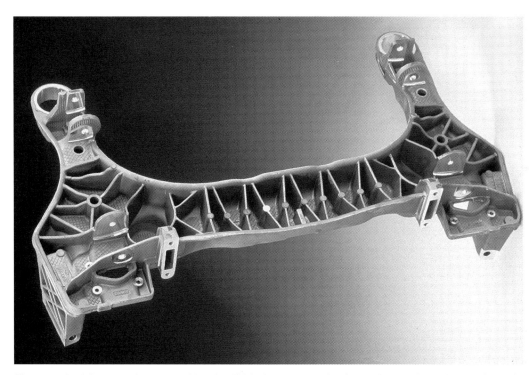

The cast aluminium crossbeam, to which the XK8's front suspension is attached, helps to isolate the main body structure from road shocks. As well as achieving better dimensional control, it also offered a considerable weight saving over a fabricated steel beam.

a spinning wheel will be braked momentarily to help restore grip. Both the TC and ASC systems can be switched off, and indeed are not recommended to be used in certain circumstances, such as when extricating the car from deep soft snow or sand. The XK8's braking system is completed by a drum-type handbrake, the release lever being low-mounted alongside the driver's seat, just inboard of the side sill.

Jurid 518 brake pads were specified for early XK8s, but these were changed to Textar 4046 pads when the front disc diameter went up to 325mm in 1999, and there was a further pad change to Jurid 620s during the 2000 model-year.

In an age when body profiles of competing cars tend to have so much in common, it is often the details which at a glance distinguish one marque from another, and one of the most visible identifying clues at the front end of the XK8 is provided by the pair of light units which, behind their multi-curvature lenses, house the headlight main and dipped beams, the sidelights and the direction indicators. Neatly recessed into the lower edge of these lenses are the optional

headlamp washers, mounted behind plated covers, which extend forwards to expose the sprays when activated by the driver. A similarly curved theme has been adopted for the XK8's rear-light clusters.

Elliptical intake with splitter bar offers E-type echo

The plated horizontal bar across the centre of the elliptical air intake provides an echo of the front of the original E-type except that in place of the central motif there are a pair of vertical buffers, a necessary adornment in order to provide a measure of bodywork protection and to enable the car to meet impact regulations. The circular Jaguar identity badge is mounted centrally on the surrounding bodywork, the traditional jaguar head peering out of the green centre circle, surrounding which is a circular black band carrying the words 'JAGUAR' and '4 LITRE' at the top and bottom, respectively. Although some prototypes carried a similar badge on the bootlid, this was omitted from production cars, which carry just the words 'JAGUAR' and 'XK8' below the left and right light clusters.

Interior provides blend of GT and sports car features

Great care was taken to provide an interior which combined the level of comfort and convenience demanded by buyers of high-performance sports and GT cars with an environment which majored on Jaguar's traditionally effective use of wood and leather. The result was a cockpit which appealed equally to customers who had been weaned off the XJS, which after its faltering start had been developed into a most effective and widely respected GT car, and to the younger but equally affluent buyer who craved a return to the better features of the E-type cockpit, but with none of its shortcomings such as inadequate space and ventilation.

Certainly the driver behind the wheel of an XK8 is confronted with an attractively and conveniently presented instrument and control layout. Immediately ahead, on one side of the full-width highly polished wood-capped facia panel, are the three main dials, deeply recessed, with the central speedometer flanked by the rev-counter on one side and combined fuel contents and water temperature gauges on the other. The centre section of the facia also carries three dials, smaller in diameter, in a line below the two largest of the four manually adjustable intakes (the other two intakes being in the corners of the facia) of the fully automatic climate control system. The centrally placed clock is accompanied by an oil pressure gauge on one side and a battery charge indicator on the other.

The main control panel is a multi-switch arrangement in three levels set above the chosen in-car entertainment equipment and housed in a console which also wraps round the transmission lever with its J-gate channel. Further finger-tip controls are mounted on each side of the steering wheel pad, one set handling the cruise control and fuel computer functions and the other the audio equipment, while the screen wash/wipe, optional headlamp washers and the lights controls are mounted on steering

Standard equipment for the XK8 includes 17in diameter wheels all round, this being the Lamina design, which for the 2000 model year replaced the five-spoke design seen at the car's launch.

The front-hinged engine cover, which is released from inside the car, is supported when raised by twin struts. Although the compartment is quite crowded, routine checks of fluid levels are easy.

column stalks.

On the car's introduction, there were 11 external colours from which to choose, while the standard interior included a choice of

Classic and Sport interiors offer best of both worlds

Oatmeal or Charcoal cloth upholstery, black carpets and Charcoal door trim panels and facia. But two grades of leather interior were also offered, identified as Classic and Sport; subsequently, the latter was to become part of the car's standard specification. The Classic treatment, involving the use of burr walnut on the facia, with a matching transmission selector knob and the top and bottom segments of the otherwise leather-covered steering wheel, came with the choice of Oatmeal, Charcoal, Cream or Teal leather. With the Sport interior, for which the wood was maple and both the transmission knob and steering wheel were fully leather-covered – although a wood and leather-rimmed wheel was a further option – the upholstery choice was between Oatmeal, Charcoal and Cream.

Each of these optional interior packs offered an abundance of Connolly leather covering the upholstery and interior trim. Controls for the electric adjustment of the high-backed front seats were recessed into the front outer corners of the cushion, and supplementary manually operated backrest releases were provided in the sides of the seat backs in order to gain access to the inevitably somewhat cramped rear seat area. This cannot be considered as anything more than accommodation for very small children or, more likely, as an additional luggage and parcels area to supplement the quite generous main luggage compartment in the rear, one of the design briefs for which had been that it had to accommodate a set of golf clubs. A remote luggage compartment release is located in the knee pad area of the facia surround on the driver's side. Controls for the electrically controlled door windows are neatly recessed into the armrest/pulls, and just forward of the interior door release lever on the driver's side are the control buttons for the seat memory when this option has been specified.

Unlike the XJS, and despite the fact that the XK8 – for reasons of engineering cost and gestation time – was required to make use of a considerable amount of its predecessor's platform and inner structural architecture, the new car was designed from the start with a structure which could be adapted to both Coupe and Convertible body styles, which nevertheless still meant that the open-topped version required special attention. But it also provided a useful yardstick for all XK8 models, for example in the performance of the body seals; every open car can be expected to have an element of flex under extreme conditions which may not be apparent in an equivalent all-metal closed body, so to achieve the required standards of rigidity, panel fit, window sealing, etc in the Convertible became the primary aim, which could then be translated into something of a bonus for the Coupe.

The quality of seals, which Jaguar developed in collaboration with the Japanese company Nippondenso, is something of which the project engineers are as proud as they are of the XK8's outstanding panel fit. Quiet running of the Convertible became a priority target, the attainment of which was assisted by the window closing arrangements whereby the door glasses, if raised, were arranged to automatically drop approximately 15mm whenever the door was opened and then to rise back into the seal channels when the door was closed again.

The soft-top, which had been developed in collaboration with the convertible experts Karmann, was fully lined on an aluminium frame and included a heated glass rear window; it can be lowered completely by holding down the control switch for approximately 20 seconds. This operation simultaneously lowers the rear quarter windows behind the doors, although these can also be adjusted independently of the top. When raised again, an operation which again takes 20 seconds, the soft-top automatically locks into position on the screen rail. Unlike on some rival cars, the lowered top is not

Although a space-saver spare wheel is standard equipment on the XK8, there is adequate under-floor space for the optional full-size 17in wheel and tyre alongside the battery.

The XK8's fuel filler cap is mounted in the left rear wing panel and is released by a cockpit-mounted control button.

hidden beneath a metal cover, but is housed beneath a separate soft tonneau cover which is attached by two press studs and two ring clips and is retained in position by the trunk lid. When not in use the tonneau is stowed in a soft bag in the luggage compartment. The bonus for this small amount of manual effort is that the Convertible has the largest luggage volume in its class at 307 litres, which is just 20 litres less than that of the Coupe.

Reversing aid gives sound of diminishing space

A popular accessory for all XK models, which was originally only available as a dealer-fit accessory, but became available as a factory-fit item on 2001 model-year cars, is a reverse parking aid, a system which operates via four ultrasonic sensors fitted across the rear bumper. When reverse gear is selected the sensors are activated and send information to a small control module located in the boot (trunk) of the car. When an obstacle is approximately 5 to 6ft away an intermittent signal is emitted from a speaker, which is hidden behind the rear seat back, the frequency of the signal increasing as the obstacle becomes closer until, when it is 8in away, the sound changes to a continuous tone. An extremely helpful aid when parking in congested places.

Another option – available across the XK range – which is aimed at the busy business user is the fixed in-car telephone system, which has been substantially upgraded for

Upgraded in-car telephone selects best frequency

the 2001 model-year. In its latest form it has 8 Watts of power (earlier installations operated with just 2 Watts) and it automatically selects either a 900MHz or

1800MHz frequency band according to local conditions.

It incorporates a filtering system which cancels out background noise, offers voice-activated dialling of up to 20 numbers, has a memo recording facility with up to 3 minutes' memory, and a data port which allows information to be transferred to and from a laptop PC (via an RS232 lead) at 14.4 KB per second. The telephone is fully integrated with the car's audio system and multi-function steering wheel, the handset is concealed inside the centre console and the antenna is hidden within the rear bumper. An additional accessory is a charging port, located in the passenger's glove box, enabling personal portable phones to be charged independently of the fixed phone system.

The optional headlamp power wash operates from a telescopic mounting which when not in operation is hidden behind a triangular plate recessed into the bottom of the lamp clusters.

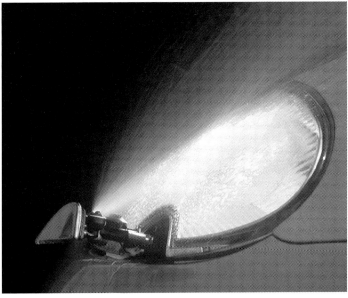

CHAPTER 6

ENTER THE XKR

Supercharging the performance

It was inevitable that sooner or later there would be a hotter version of XK8, and the form that such a car would take was clearly flagged in 1997 when an XJR version of the XJ8 saloon emerged featuring a supercharged version of the 4-litre V8 engine, various associated mechanical upgrades and the inevitable cosmetic changes for model-identity purposes.

It was not until 1998 that a similar treatment was applied to the XK8, and there was considerable pent-up demand for it by the time of its launch, which once again took place in Geneva during what coincidentally was the 50th anniversary year of the original XK120. This time there was a little less euphoria at the unveiling because the XKR had been so widely anticipated, although if

The mesh grille and these standard 18in Double Five alloy wheels immediately distinguish the XKR from a standard-specification XK8.

The excellent fit of the Karmann-developed soft top is a major contributor to the great popularity of the Convertible, particularly in the US market.

anything there was even more eagerness to get behind the wheel to find out just what the uprated specification translated to on the road.

Like the XK8, the XKR was to be offered in both Coupe and Convertible versions and, rather as anticipated, the uprated models traded just a touch of the 'standard' cars' soft-riding character for the robust performance that an additional 80bhp could provide. Jaguar selected the Eaton M112 supercharger – incorporating twin air-to-coolant intercoolers – for the XKR, and at the same time the air intake system was modified to incorporate two resonators to reduce external noise levels as well as to further improve cabin refinement, the exhaust system also undergoing detail changes internally to the same end.

The supercharged engine operated at a compression ratio of 9:1, resulting in a maximum power output of 370bhp at 6,150rpm, a 28 per cent increase over the XK8's figure, while torque had gone up up by 33 per cent to 387lb.ft at 3,600rpm, which meant that the XK8's ZF transmission could not be transferred into the XKR. Instead, the Mercedes-Benz WA580 five-speed transmission was chosen, suitably modified to accept the Jaguar J-gate gear selection, and the drive from it continues to the differential via a two-piece propshaft. The transmission ratios with this installation are 3.59, 2.19, 1.41, 1.00 and 0.83:1, in other words little changed from the ZF ratios in the XK8, while the same final-drive ratio of 3.06:1 has been retained.

Minor recalibration of the engine management system and the transmission control module was made to suit the XKR application. The ZF Servotronic power steering also underwent further development to provide greater electronic adjustability, recalibration of the ECU having provided more weighting at the wheel at higher speeds and improved feel in the straight-ahead position, while the steering rack mounts were stiffened.

Along with the increased engine performance came an increase in stopping power, the front brake disc diameter being increased from the XK8's 305mm to 325mm, although these larger diameter discs were to be standardized across the XK range from 1999. Initially supplied with Textar 4046 brake pads, the XKR went over to Jurid 620 pads for the 2000 model-year cars, while Brembo brakes *(described in more detail later)* became an option available through Jaguar's Special Vehicles office in Brown's Lane from mid-1999.

Higher XKR prices offset by extra standard equipment

Although at the time of launch the £59,300 UK price of an XKR Coupe and £66,300 for the Convertible represented a premium of £9,350 over the cost of the equivalent XK8 models, £4,000 of this was accounted for by equipment which was only optional on the XK8 but standard on the XKR. This included the Computer Active Technology Suspension (CATS) with Bilstein dampers, the Sport leather interior pack with combined wood-and-leather steering wheel and wooden gear knob, a trunk-mounted six-disc CD autochanger, cruise control, powered fold-back exterior mirrors and the headlamp power wash.

In addition, one of the easiest ways of distinguishing an XKR from an XK8 has been by the supercharged car's unique and extremely attractive 10-spoke alloy wheels which, like a CATS-equipped XK8, carry 18in diameter Pirelli P Zero tyres, directional 245/45s at the front and assymetric 255/45s at the rear, on 8in and 9in rims, respectively.

The additional heat generated by the supercharged engine called for twin louvred inserts in the engine compartment cover, the modified airflow resulting from these being compensated for by the addition of a small integral spoiler on the trailing edge of the luggage compartment lid. From the front an

The engine compartment of the XKR revealing the smoothly contoured top covers of the V8 power unit. Performance and emissions levels of the supercharged engine were improved in 2000 with the aid of a revised management system allowing electronic throttle movement and cruise control and incorporating an oil temperature sensor, while gas vapour was drawn away from the exhaust manifold and back into the throttle body for recombustion.

Twin extractor vents in the front bodywork are necessary to allow temperatures in the engine compartment of the supercharged XKR to be maintained at a satisfactory level, the cars' aerodynamic balance being restored by the addition of a small spoiler on the boot (trunk) lid.

XKR is also identifiable by its stainless steel mesh grille which fills the oval air intake. Like the XK8 models, the XKR Coupes and Convertibles are also candidates for a series of R Performance option packs *(see sidebar in next Chapter for details)* which sharpen up their dynamic qualities even more as well as giving them a distinct visual identity.

Road-testers were almost unanimous in their praise for the XKR when it first appeared in its regular specification and drew some interesting comparisons with the XK8. Predictably, with such abundant torque, the curve for which peaks at 3,600rpm instead of at 4,250rpm, the XKR fairly rockets away from rest, while at the top end the additional 80bhp enables it to sustain crisp acceleration right through to its electronically limited top speed of 155mph. The more immediate response to throttle-pedal kickdown was commented on favourably, while the extra weighting of the XKR's steering also earned wide praise for having given the car genuine sports car agility.

When *Autocar* decided to conduct a comparison test with an XKR Convertible, they chose a 3.4-litre Porsche 911 Cabriolet for 'opposition' and found that the Jaguar

Jaguar on top for refinement and ride quality

out-performed it by a small margin throughout the acceleration tests to 130mph despite a weight penalty of approximately 250kg. Predictably, the Jaguar also scored heavily on both refinement and on the quality of ride from the uprated suspension.

XKR SILVERSTONE
A limited edition is a concept that one normally associates with high-volume

The different wheel rim widths – 8in at the front, 9in at the rear – mean that all XKRs must be supplied with a space-saver spare wheel. Standard equipment on XKRs also includes electrochromic and power-folding exterior mirrors and rain-sensing screen wipers, the latter also becoming standard on XK8s in 2000.

Celebrating Jaguar's return to the race tracks and entry into Formula One, the XKR Silverstone has most of the XKR's R Performance options, including the distinctive 20in diameter split-rim Detroit wheels from BBS – though finished in silver rather than the usual gold – as part of the standard package.

Like the Silverstone Coupe, the Convertible has a limited production run of just 50 examples, all of them finished in Platinum silver; all the Convertibles are equipped with a black top.

manufacturers, who periodically 'dress up' their mainstream models to give them a little more sales impetus in their mid life, but the idea of the XKR Silverstone is very different. In the words of Jaguar's managing director Jonathan Browning at the time of the car's launch in April 2000: 'This year marks a new chapter in Jaguar's racing history. The XKR Silverstone is a celebration not only of Jaguar's return to racing through Formula One, but of our long association with the world-famous British circuit, the scene of over 20 Jaguar racing victories. But above all the XKR Silverstone, with its supercharged engine, finely tuned chassis and distinctive style, is a sports car for the true driving enthusiast.'

Just 100 examples of the Silverstone were to be built, 50 Coupes and 50 Convertibles, all of them finished in Platinum Silver, with a few exclusive modifications to the Sports interior, and in the case of the Convertibles all with a black top. The Silverstone differs from the regular XKR in 'borrowing' from Jaguar's R Performance options catalogue a set of 20in diameter BBS Detroit five-spoke split-rim alloy wheels equipped with ultra-low profile Pirelli P Zero tyres, 255/35s on 9in wide rims at the front and 285/30s on 10in rims at the rear. Mounted inboard of

20-inch wheels the largest yet seen on a production Jaguar

them are a set of the higher-performance Brembo brakes referred to above, using 355mm diameter and 32mm wide two-piece ventilated and cross-drilled discs at the front and single-piece discs 330mm diameter by 28mm wide at the rear. The brakes, which were developed jointly by Brembo and Jaguar, are operated through silver-finished four-piston aluminium calipers which carry the Jaguar logo in red. The wheels, which are also silver-finished, and are the largest ever fitted to a Jaguar production car, and the uprated brakes were first displayed in public

on the XK180 concept car designed and engineered by Jaguar's Special Vehicle Operations, which made its debut at the Paris motor show in 1998 *(see Chapter 9)*.

The 50 Silverstone Coupes (but not the Convertibles) also benefit from SVO's R Performance Handling Pack, within which the electronic control unit and damper settings of the CATS system have been recalibrated for more taut handling, while

Silverstone Coupes given recalibrated R-Performance Pack

the springs and anti-roll bars are uprated for increased roll stiffness. The variable-ratio, speed-sensitive power steering system has also been retuned for enhanced precision and feel.

Apart from the wheels, Silverstone models can be identified by 'JAGUAR SILVERSTONE' badges at front and rear in which the familiar jaguar 'growler' head appears out of a black background surrounded by a silver band carrying the 'JAGUAR' and 'SILVERSTONE' words in red. The words are also repeated on the chrome kickplates attached to the body sills.

Inside the car, there are sports seats trimmed in Warm Charcoal leather with red stitching, 'smoke' stained bird's-eye maple facia veneer carrying a 'SILVERSTONE' identity, and the car is fitted with Jaguar's premium in-car entertainment equipment with multiple speakers and a six-disc CD autochanger system. Other minor touches are the red piping for the carpets and red stitching on the steering wheel. In addition to the inclusion of the above-mentioned identification features, the announcement of the Silverstone gave customers the opportunity to buy an XKR which had already been loaded with virtually all of the available R Performance options as part of a standard package for a total price no greater than if the items in question had been selected individually from the options catalogue.

The distinctive interior of the XKR Silverstone includes red stitching to the Warm Charcoal-finished upholstery and steering wheel and Smoke-stained bird's eye maple veneer on the facia.

This special badge on the nose identifies the XKR Silverstone and further identity is provided on the facia and on the tread plates covering the body sills.

XKR models carry a nose badge with a red surround to the jaguar growler and lettering which confirms that the 4-litre engine is supercharged.

The XKR Silverstone went on sale in the UK at a price of £66,785 for the Coupe and £72,185 for the Convertible, after which the only remaining options were a DVD-ROM satellite navigation system and an integrated GSM phone system.

In a less demanding setting, this XKR Convertible with its optional R Performance 20in Detroit wheels, and uprated Brembo brakes, steering and suspension, is virtually up to Silverstone specification and demonstrated electrifying acceleration when the opportunity occurred.

An XKR Silverstone Convertible being taken to the limit during a demonstration on the circuit that gave the car its model name.

CHAPTER 7

IMPROVING THE PRODUCT

Running changes and upgrades

Like virtually every series-production car that has ever been built, the XK8 and XKR models have been the subject of a steady flow of running changes in specification since the first models were introduced in 1996. This is all part of the normal car-manufacturing process, and many of these changes did not warrant or receive press announcements at the time. Nevertheless, knowledge of the more significant of them can be valuable for anyone who either owns or – perhaps more importantly – is contemplating the purchase of a previously owned car, which may or may not have benefited from some of the specification upgrades. The following, therefore, is a list of the more important changes and identification features which have taken place from the 1998 model-year onwards and a fuller description of some of the more recent of them.

1998 MY
- Auto headlamps became standard in all markets except those which took daytime running lamps (Canada, Chile, Denmark. Finland, Norway and Sweden).

- Revised instrument pack graphics.

- Electrochromatic interior mirror became standard in all markets.

1999 MY
- Rear bootlid badge deleted.

- Cloth door pad on Sport trim interiors replaced by ambla.

- Front footwell mats have 'Jaguar' rather than 'XK8' encrypted in the heel piece to coincide with introduction of the XKR.

- XKR front disc brake diameter increased from 305 to 325mm.

- Servotronic II power steering introduced on XKR, then standard across XK range (XK8 tuned lighter).

- Servotronic II 'Sport' fitted as standard to all CATS vehicles.

- AJ27 engine replaced AJ26 with the following key upgrades:
  Air assist injectors.
  Continuously variable cam phasing.
  Revised EMS.
  Modified pistons.
  Oil temperature sensing.
  New electronic throttle.
  Revised cruise control.
  Double-plated platinum spark plugs.
  North American Onboard Refuelling Vapour Recovery System (ORVR).

- AJ26 supercharged engine introduced in Japan (was originally released on XKR at 1998½ MY in UK, European and other overseas markets).

- Revised 5W/30 engine oil used.

- Instrument pack returned to 1997 MY condition with addition of brighter white ink and pale blue compensation layer.

A contrast in styles. Although subtle variations in seat design have been an ongoing development for the XK8, in year 2000 there was still a choice between the Classic and Sport interior packs. Apart from their lighter colour, the Classic leather seats still have fore-and-aft fluting whereas the latest Sport seats have curved flutes in place of the earlier straight-across style.

Subtle changes to the exterior of the 2001-model XK8 Coupe include a chromed bootlid plinth with the Jaguar name embossed in it, chromed surrounds to the revised jewel-effect rear light clusters and a modified rear bumper cover.

These three wheels are amongst the performance options which have been offered for the XK Jaguars. From the top, the 18in Milan, the 20in Paris and the 20in Detroit wheels, the last two being split-rim designs.

- Motorola Startac 85 GSM telephone replaced Motorola 8700 series.

- Newly approved accessories:
  Reversing aid.
  Boot rack.
  Pollen filters.
  Chrome number-plate plinth.
  Boot liner.
  'Spike Spider' 16in, 17in and 18in snow chains.
  Alpine PS Navigation System.

- Service interval for double-plated platinum spark plugs increased in September 1998 from 60,000 to 70,000 miles (normally aspirated engines only).

2000 MY

- XK8 17in Revolver wheels replaced with Lamina style.

- Seatbelt pre-tensioners became electronically instead of mechanically fired.

- Seatbelt webbing with 'closed-loop' edge within the weave of the material.

- Boot stowage net fitted as standard (flat accessory net still available as an accessory).

- Adaptive Cruise Control introduced on XKR for UK/Europe.

- Traction Control fitted as standard in North America (previously a cost option and Stability Control as standard).

- ABS *plus* introduced.

- AJ27 supercharged engine introduced.

- Integrated navigation system introduced.

- Rain sensing wipers fitted.

- Base in-car entertainment sound system with six (previously four) speakers.

- Premium in-car entertainment system uses 320W Alpine Premium (previously 240W Harman Kardon).

- CD Autochanger fitted as standard on all XK series.

- Encrypted key transponder has rolling algorithm code.

- New VIN number prefix identification code.

2001 MY
- Adaptive Restraint Technology System (ARTS) as standard on all XK cars.

- Dual-band fixed in-car telephone optional on all XK series with automatic selection of 900MHz or 1800MHz frequency bands according to local conditions.

- Two new seat styles, both with leather trim as standard; Classic five-flute design standard on XK8, embossed Sport design standard on XKR and optional on XK8.

- 12-way electrical adjustment of driver's and passenger's seats.

- Adjustable head restraints which automatically retract when seat backs are tilted forward for easier access to rear compartment, then resume their preset height as seats are repositioned for use.

- Side airbags mounted in bolsters of seats.

- New 'comfort system' seat belts with dual-stage spring mechanism allowing less tension on chest and shoulder after retraction is completed and buckle has been engaged for normal usage.

- New 'mood' lighting offering improved after-dark visibility of interior.

- Jewel-effect tail-lamps with chrome surrounds.

- New front bumper cover on all XK models and new splitter bar on the XK8.

- New rear bumper cover incorporating concealed screw-in towing eye.

- New chrome bootlid plinth embossed with 'JAGUAR' and incorporating integral electric boot-release button depicting the jaguar 'growler' emblem.

- Tailpipe finishers on XKR.

- Flusher-fitting front foglamps.

The 17in Lamina wheel, which replaced the Revolver type as standard equipment on XK8s for the 2000 model year.

Further distinguishing items of 2001-model XK8s include the more prominent foglamps and slightly changed bumper cover and splitter bar. This Coupe is equipped with the 18" Impeller wheels.

The drilled discs of the Brembo brakes, which come as part of the R Performance package with gold-finished 20in Detroit wheels, are clearly visible behind the five slim spokes.

The optional R Performance Brembo brakes feature four-piston aluminium calipers front and rear with ventilated and cross-drilled two-piece front and single-piece rear discs.

In addition to uprated wheels and brakes, Coupe models are also available with a handling pack incorporating CATS, which involves revised electronic control unit and damper settings, uprated springs and anti-roll bars and a retuned variable-ratio, speed-sensitive steering system.

R Performance options for the XK8

In September 1999, Jaguar revealed details of a series of R Performance options for its production cars which had been developed by Jaguar Special Vehicle Operations (SVO), the company's specialist in-house design and engineering department, and were to be made available either as factory-fit options or as dealer-fit accessories. Comprising a series of Handling Packs involving a choice of BBS alloy wheels, uprated Brembo brakes and suspension upgrades, the options offered for the XK8 (with the UK retail prices at time of introduction appended) were as follows:

XK8 Convertible

BBS Milan alloy wheels, 8.5in x 18in front, 9in x 18in rear, with 245/45 and 255/45 tyres (£1,950).

BBS Milan alloy wheels, 8.5in x 18in front, 9in x 18in rear, with 245/45 and 255/45 tyres, including CATS (£2,750).

BBS Paris or Detroit alloy wheels, 9in x 20in front, 10in x 20in rear, with 255/35 and 285/30 tyres (£2,950).

BBS Paris or Detroit alloy wheels, 9in x 20in front, 10in x 20in rear, with 255/35 and 285/30 tyres, including CATS (£3,750).

Brembo brakes, BBS Milan alloy wheels, 8.5in x 18in front, 9in x 18in rear, with 245/45 and 255/45 tyres and BBS space-saver spare wheel (£3,800).

Brembo brakes, BBS Milan alloy wheels, 8.5in x 18in front, 9in x 18in rear, with 245/45 and 255/45 tyres, including CATS, and BBS space-saver spare wheel (£4,600).

Brembo brakes, BBS Paris or Detroit alloy wheels, 9in x 20in front, 10in x 20in rear, with 255/35 and 285/30 tyres and BBS space-saver spare wheel (£4,800).

Brembo brakes, BBS Paris or Detroit alloy wheels, 9in x 20in front, 10in x 20in rear, with 255/35 and 285/30 tyres, including CATS, and BBS space-saver spare wheel (£5,100).

XK8 Coupe

As XK8 Convertible plus:
Brembo brakes and Handling Pack with CATS, BBS Milan alloy wheels, 8.5in x 18in front, 9in x 18in rear, with 245/45 and 255/45 tyres and BBS space-saver spare wheel (£6,200).

Brembo brakes and Handling Pack with CATS, BBS Paris or Detroit alloy wheels, 9in x 20in front, 10in x 20in rear, with 255/35 and 285/30 tyres and BBS space-saver spare wheel (£7,200).

- New 18in Impeller wheels with seven double-edge spokes as option on XK8 but standard on cars equipped with CATS.

- 17in Lamina wheels as standard on XK8 and 18in Double Five wheels on XKR.

- Previous dealer-fit reverse-parking also offered as a line-fit option.

- Enhanced features for Adaptive Cruise Control.

Adaptive Restraint Technology System (ARTS)

Introduced as standard on all XK models for the 2001 model year, Jaguar are claiming ARTS to be the world's most comprehensive and sophisticated ultrasonic occupant safety sensing system for cars. Four ultrasonic sensors, located in the A-pillar, the B-pillar and in a modified roof console, are used to determine the presence and position of the front seat passenger's head and upper torso in relation to the passenger airbag deployment door. If the passenger is too close to the facia the airbag will not deploy and a warning light will illuminate to indicate that the passenger airbag is inactive. As soon as the passenger moves far enough away from the facia the airbag becomes active again and the warning light is extinguished. There is also a weight sensor in the front passenger seat which detects the presence and approximate weight of the occupant in order to determine whether and to what extent the airbag should be deployed. For the driver, an electronic sensor in the seat track measures the distance between the driver's seat and the steering wheel and

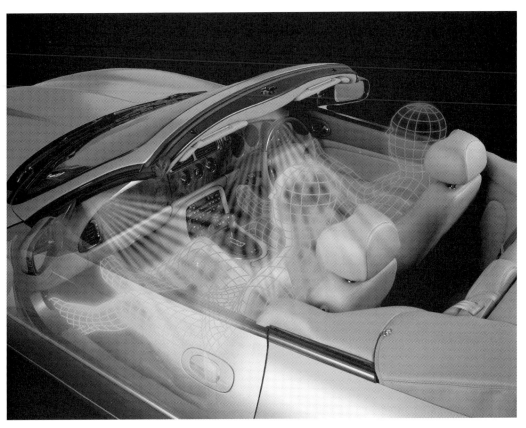

Jaguar's latest Adaptive Restraint Technology System, which monitors the position of the driver in relation to the steering wheel, also whether or not the passenger seat is in use, and if so the weight of the occupant, all so as to ensure the safest possible deployment of airbags in a crash situation.

R Performance options for the XKR

Although the XKR is already considerably uprated in specification and performance compared with the XK8, Jaguar also offers a series of further upgrades in the form of R Performance options for either factory fitment or as dealer-fit accessories, as follows (UK prices at launch time in September 1999 are quoted):

XKR Convertible
BBS Milan alloy wheels, 8.5in x 18in front, 9in x 18in rear, with 245/45 and 255/45 tyres (£1,450).

BBS Paris or Detroit alloy wheels, 9in x 20in front, 10in x 20in rear, with 255/35 and 285/30 tyres (£2,450).

Brembo brakes, BBS Milan alloy wheels, 8.5in x 18in front, 9in x 18in rear, with 245/45 and 255/45 tyres and BBS space-saver spare wheel (£3,300).

Brembo brakes, BBS Paris or Detroit alloy wheels, 9in x 20in front, 10in x 20in rear, with 255/35 and 285/30 tyres and BBS space-saver spare wheel (£4,300).

XKR Coupe
As XKR Convertible plus:
Brembo brakes and Handling Pack, BBS Milan alloy wheels, 8.5in x 18in front, 9in x 18in rear, with 245/45 and 255/45 tyres and BBS space-saver spare wheel (£4,900).

Brembo brakes and Handling Pack, BBS Paris or Detroit alloy wheels, 9in x 20in front, 10in x 20in rear, with 255/35 and 285/30 tyres and BBS space-saver spare wheel (£5,900).

Optional navigation equipment in close-up showing the two rows of control buttons flanking the central screen. Country-scanning DVD discs are available for most European countries.

further sensors in the seatbelt buckles for both seats alert the system to whether or not each seat is occupied, while crash sensors on the front crossmember panel and at the sides of the car gauge the severity of an impact.

Each sensor feeds information to the system's central processor, which governs the use of seatbelt pretensioners and the deployment of the dual-stage front airbags, which are inflated fully or partially according to the occupant data and the severity of the impact. The system is claimed to be especially beneficial for smaller front-seat occupants, particularly in low-speed collisions which do not necessitate airbag inflation at full force. Decisions are computed in as little as 10 milliseconds, or about 25 times faster than the blink of an eye.

In installing ARTS, modifications have been made to XK bodyshells, including reinforcement of the front side members which not only provide additional rigidity, but also allow the sensors to be positioned so that an impact can be detected as quickly and accurately as possible. The driver's airbag incorporates a star-fold pattern allowing radial deployment to reduce the risk of airbag-induced injuries to a driver seated too close to the wheel, while the latest front seats incorporate side airbags for head and ribcage protection in severe side impacts.

Adaptive Cruise Control (ACC)

Using microwave radar technology, ACC was originally introduced in September 1999 as an option on the XKR in the UK and Germany before becoming available on the XK8 from the end of 2000. In the meantime, the system has been upgraded in several ways. Measuring 14 x 10 x 7cm and weighing just 870gm, the latest sensor is some 60% smaller and 1,300gm lighter than the earlier model and makes 40 individual measurement beams on each horizontal scan.

The system eliminates the need for the driver to adjust the set speed or to disengage cruise control in order to avoid encroaching on slower-moving traffic ahead. Instead, by automatically adjusting the throttle and, if necessary, applying limited braking, ACC maintains a constant time gap to the vehicle in front as well as allowing the car to cruise at a preset speed if the lane ahead is empty. The set speed is permanently displayed in the instrument cluster, and a 'Sensor Blocked'

An XKR Coupe with adaptive cruise control, which was introduced as an XKR option in September 1999 and became available for the XK8 from the end of 2000. In its latest form ACC displays the set speed permanently in the instrument cluster and a 'Sensor Blocked' message should the 40-beam radar scan become obstructed by a build-up of snow or mud.

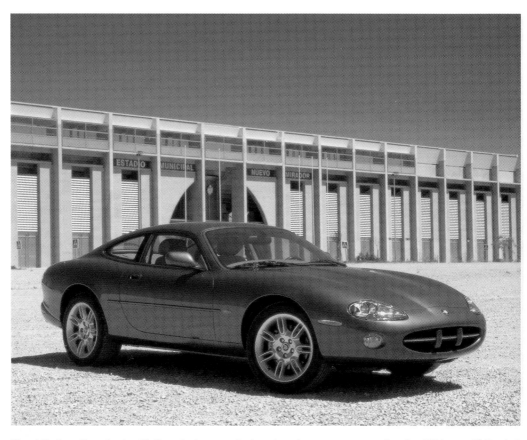

The 18in Impeller wheel, with its set of seven dual spokes, became a new option for 2001-year XK8s, but standard equipment on cars equipped with the CATS suspension.

message will appear there if the radar sensor should become blocked by, for example, an accumulation of mud or snow at the front of the car.

Colour and trim combinations

Jaguar has long had a policy of offering the widest possible range of exterior paintwork, soft-top and interior trim colours, and nowhere has this been more apparent than within the XK series. In many instances, colours have been offered for the Coupe and/or Convertible specifically in response to a request from a particular market, and the resulting combination may well be exclusive to that one country, while the total number of colour combinations which have been offered throughout the world since XK8 production began is almost countless.

Equally confusing, some Jaguar colours carry exotic names which are of limited value in indicating the actual colour involved. For example, when the XK8 was launched in

October 1996 for the 1997 model-year the 11 exterior colours on offer were Aquamarine, Topaz, British Racing Green, Sherwood Green, Anthracite, Carnival, Spindrift, Antigua, Sapphire, Titanium and Ice Blue, and a year later the last two were replaced by Meteorite and Amaranth.

The XKR colour choices were initially limited to eight, these being British Racing Green, Amaranth, Carnival, Sherwood Green, Antigua, Sapphire, Anthracite and Phoenix Red, the latter having replaced Aquamarine during 1998. Phoenix Red also became available on the XK8 from the 1999 model-year, at which point Sherwood Green was dropped, Spindrift and Alpine were added (but for the XK8 only) and Meteorite and Topaz were added to the XKR colours. Cashmere was now a fifth trim option for all XK models.

There were even more changes for the 2000 model-year, Antigua, Phoenix Red, Meteorite and Amaranth all being deleted

More performance from Paramount

Any observant car-spotter in the UK who has spied an XK8 or an XKR brandishing bodywork and/or interior changes, or perhaps has identified a different exhaust note, has almost certainly been looking at and/or listening to one of the bespoke vehicles produced by Paramount Performance, of Beaconsfield, Buckinghamshire.

Paramount, who acquired the rights to the Chasseur marque and product range in 1996, and in 1998 became the official UK importer for the German Jaguar conversion specialist Arden, are now in the business of developing performance, handling and styling equipment for Jaguar (and Daimler) models which have been produced during the 1990s, and at the time of writing they have applied these to more than 50 cars in the XK range.

The company's system conversions, which involve changes to the bodywork, engine, transmission, suspension, steering and brakes as well as interior decor and equipment, have been assembled in various groupings to create four different models into which a production XK8 or XKR can be converted, two of these being listed as Sport, and the other two as De Luxe models.

The flagship of the Paramount range is undoubtedly the XKR 450 Grand Prix, a model which is instantly identifiable by its carbon fibre and aluminium bodywork panelling, which at the front incorporates a wide oval grille above a three-intake airdam, and at the rear by a bootlid spoiler.

Mirroring Jaguar's own development of the XJ-V8 engine for installation in the XK180 concept car *(see Chapter 9)*, Paramount's 450 Grand Prix benefits from a 10 per cent increase in supercharger speed and revisions have also been made to the induction system, the intercooling has been improved and a special exhaust system has been fitted. The car's suspension has been lowered by 30mm and uprated shock absorbers and revised suspension bushes have replaced the standard items.

One of the most intriguing changes in the Grand Prix has followed Paramount's acquisition in 1998 of the world rights to Racelogic's steering wheel control system for Jaguar automatic gearboxes, which is being marketed under the F1 SwitchShift

The XKR 450 is the flagship of the Paramount Performance range of converted XK-series Jaguars.

This is the XK8 Burnham, for which the bodywork changes are produced in polyester rather than the carbon fibre and aluminium used for the more expensive models.

label and is operated through buttons on the back of the steering wheel. The car sits on a set of 19in split-rim wheels shod with 255mm front and 285mm rear tyres, and inboard of them are a set of uprated brakes, while the steering has been given a switchable servo feel. The Grand Prix also has what Paramount describes as their metal components pack, which includes aluminium pedal set and foot support, instrument surround rings and gearlever, the latter with a chromium plated surround, and the cockpit air vents are also plated.

The Grosvenor is the Grand Prix's opposite number in the De Luxe range, with similar changes to the bodywork, transmission, suspension and steering, but with different 19in wheels and the engine alterations being confined to a revised stainless large-bore exhaust system with a choice of sports tones.

At £29,450 and £26,900, respectively, on top of the cost of the standard car, the XKR 450 Grand Prix and the Grosvenor are not exactly budget-priced items, but there is a lower-cost alternative to each of them. On the Sport side there is the Donington, for which the bodywork changes are moulded in polyester and there is a choice between one 18in and two 19in sets of wheels and tyres, plus the lowered suspension, the revised large-bore exhaust system, the switchable steering and a Sports interior pack. Its opposite number on the De Luxe side is the Burnham, which retains the standard Jaguar exhaust with large tail trims and has a different interior pack with special leather trim. Depending on the choice of wheels and tyres, the Donington conversion costs from £10,450 to £14,400 and the Burnham from £12,750 to £14,950.

However, the four complete cars are only part of the Paramount conversion story because virtually every item fitted to one or other of them, plus many other bespoke parts ranging from three-eared wheel spinners to a hardtop for Convertibles, plus a wide variety of alternative interior treatments, are also available individually on an options list from which XK8 and XKR owners can tailor their car to their particular taste. In this instance, conversion work or fitment is carried out either at Paramount's own premises or by arrangement through selected Jaguar dealerships, while easy-to-fit items are sold mail-order direct to owners.

and Platinum, Jupiter Red and Pacific Blue added to the list, while four colours already being offered on other Jaguars – Westminster, Seafrost, Titanium and Mistral – along with newcomer Emerald were also extended to the XK range, while inside the car the Teal leather option was replaced by Nimbus.

The hood (soft-top) colour options for Convertibles have varied according to the chosen exterior and interior colour combinations for the car concerned, but overall there has been the option of five different hood colour finishes – black, green, blue, dark beige and light beige. During the 1999 model-year there were no fewer than 68 choices of hood/interior trim, while for the 2000 model-year this had grown to 110 different combinations.

For 2001 model-year cars there have been two further changes of exterior colour,

Spindrift and Alpine having been replaced by White Onyx and Roman Bronze. These have joined Anthracite, Westminster, Sapphire, Pacific, Mistral, Phoenix, Carnival, Seafrost, British Racing Green, Emerald, Topaz, Platinum and Titanium to make 15 choices for XK cars in all markets outside of North America.

For this territory, just four colours were being offered across the full four-car range of two Coupes and two Convertibles – Anthracite, Phoenix, British Racing Green and Platinum. Both the Convertibles were also being listed in White Onyx or Titanium, the XK8 Coupe in Carnival and Topaz, and the XK8 Convertible in all these colours plus Pacific and Roman Bronze. The 15 exterior colours and five choices of interior trim were again being linked to a selection of five hood colours, making a total of 109 different choices, just one less than the previous year.

The interior of an XK8 equipped with the optional Sport Pack which for 2001 includes redesigned seats offering more support and longer cushions.

CHAPTER 8

BEHIND THE WHEEL

XK8 and XKR on test

The period immediately after the launch of a totally new car, which has involved the expenditure of many millions of pounds or dollars and has occupied many of a manufacturer's key technical personnel for several years, is always an anxious time. The launch is one thing – this is when style is pre-eminent, and when performance on the road has to be taken for granted, at least for the time being – but professional analysis by road-testers is what in the end will influence potential buyers most of all and determine whether or not the manufacturer concerned has produced a winner.

The first road-test reports of the XK8 were not long in appearing, and almost without exception they brought good news. Inevitably, there were a few minor quibbles – some testers found that the seats and their range of adjustments were not entirely to their liking; others, when they tried the Convertible, felt that these days not only the raising and lowering, but also the stowage and covering of a soft-top should be a totally electrically controlled operation without the driver having to move a limb other than to operate a switch; while those who habitually seem to assess the cornering power of a production car by standards more appropriate to the race track were inclined to suggest that even with the optional uprated suspension the XK8 was still a bit on the soft side. But none of the respected journals could find so much as a single fundamental flaw, and the concensus was that Jaguar and their technical collaborators had got it just about right – the XK8, they agreed, was a great car.

More than four years on from its launch, these early opinions have been largely maintained in subsequent test reports, and there can have been few if any other cars in this sector of the market which have benefited from such sustained praise during what is now quite a long period. And justifiably so because to get behind the wheel of an XK8 is, if one can be forgiven for using a well-worn cliche, to enjoy a rare driving experience. This is not occasioned by exceptional performance in any one department, such as blistering acceleration, leech-like grip, kart-sharp steering or

Successful marriage of V8 engine and automatic transmission

seatbelt-straining braking, but by the seamless welding together of very high standards of performance in every department. The success of the XK8 lies in the fact that this has been achieved in such a compatable manner as to produce a sports/GT car that is intensely satisfying and enjoyable to drive.

Quite rightly, much favourable comment has been made about the successful marriage of the 4-litre aluminium V8 engine to the ZF

More than four years after the XK8's launch, the svelte lines of this Coupe still proved to be a centre of attraction whenever the car was parked.

Rear-seat accommodation in a Coupe is inevitably restricted, but it can still be contemplated by adults for short journeys or for long runs with small children.

five-speed automatic transmission, and in particular about how the electronic control of the latter seems to have been endowed with the brain of a highly skilled driver by the manner in which it will select another gear, either up or down, at just the precise moment when an accomplished and enthusiastic driver might have been reaching for the lever had the car been equipped with a manual gearbox. Another laudable function of the Electronic Control Unit is its ability to make changes of ratio so smoothly as to be almost imperceptible.

The engine is a delight, not because it gives the XK8 exceptional acceleration (although a typical 6.6sec for the 0-60mph dash is sufficiently brisk to out-perform such potential showroom rivals as the BMW 840i, Mercedes-Benz 320SL and even, when it is in automatic-transmission form, the Aston Martin DB7), but because of its rare combination of high revving ability (the red line on the rev-counter is set at 6,800rpm) and abundant low-speed torque, for which the variable cam timing can take considerable credit.

The highly respected weekly *Autocar*, in its first full road test of a Coupe, commented: 'This is an engine that loves to rev, one that feels at its most comfortable when subjected to hard work, gathering momentum from low revs, thanks to that wide spread of torque, but reserving its most inspired work for the final 2,000rpm, at which point it emits a noise that is as glorious as it is sophisticated.' Several months later, commenting on the conclusion of a 3,000-mile test, the same magazine recorded: 'The engine has impressive elasticity, and its silence and ability to pull high gears at low revs is remarkable.'

The authority of this magazine means that its comments are always scrutinized carefully by car manufacturers, so Jaguar people were understandably delighted and relieved that the XK8 had got off to such a good start with the domestic Press, but equally important, bearing in mind the importance of the US market to the new car, was the media's reaction to the XK8 on the other side of the Atlantic. The opening comments of David E Davis Jr, the experienced editor of *Automobile* magazine, must therefore have brought a glow of pride to the people back in

The electrically adjustable driver's seat is moved through three control buttons recessed into the outer front corner of the cushion and a separate manual release catch allows the backrest to tip forwards for access into the rear. New 12-way electric adjustment has been introduced on 2001 models.

Browns Lane, Coventry, for his assessment of a Convertible began with the words: 'Jaguar's new XK8 is a spectacularly good car. It is, officially, the successor to the quirky, charming and cramped XJS, but it is far more than that. It is 10 times more beautiful than the XJS, and it offers more straight-line performance, roadholding and handling that challenge everything in the category, from the Mercedes-Benz SL500 and the Lexus SC400 to its own sister ship, the Aston Martin DB7. But it is still more than the sum of those attributes: it is rolling proof that Ford's purchase of Jaguar was exactly the right thing to do, even though most of the advantages, at the moment, seem to lie at Jaguar's end of the court.'

Davis returned to the theme at the end of his assessment: 'Ford has turned Jaguar into a modern car company that produces modern cars, and it has done so with grace and sensitivity. A good deal is one in which all the participants go home at night feeling like winners, and that's the result of the Ford-Jaguar deal. Workers, managers, dealers and consumers all emerge victorious from the six-year process that culminated with the introduction of this very nice new Jaguar XK8.'

But perhaps the last words amongst the many thousands which were devoted to initial impressions and early road tests should be those of *Road & Track*, who perceptively summarized their driving impressions of an XK8 Convertible with the following thoughts: 'The Jaguar folks are careful to define the XK8 as a "luxury sports car". The term fits. The car's size, smooth ride, overall packaging and lack of a manual transmission keep it from being a sports car in the NSX or 911 sense of the term. Yet it is convincingly sporting, genuinely fast and supremely confident. It does nothing that would alienate Jaguar's existing and loyal XJS owner base, but will attract many buyers who wouldn't even consider the previous model. Perhaps it is really a strictly defined gran turismo: ideal transport when you have a long way to go, a short time to get there and want to do so in comfort and style.'

Four years on, not only are XK8 Coupes and Convertibles a relatively familiar sight on our roads, but they now need to be assessed against ever-strengthening opposition as the

relentless pursuit of performance, refinement and efficiency of luxury sports/GT cars continues unabated throughout the industry. It speaks well of the inherent quality of these Jaguars, therefore, that they still command critical acclaim, even when evaluated against considerably younger rivals.

Slipping into the cockpit of an XK8 for the first time can be a mind-blowing experience, not least because of the proliferation of buttons, knobs, switches and read-outs which have to be addressed and studied; a few minutes spent with the comprehensively written and well illustrated driver's handbook (which resides with other driver aids in a leather-covered folder which has its own stowage slot in the upper part of the glovebox) is an essential preliminary to

Triangular speakers for the audio equipment are neatly built into the front corners of the doors. Just forward of the chromed recessed door release are the two-position buttons for the driver's seat memory.

The long doors make entry to and exit from the cockpit an easy matter and the red warning light let into the trailing edge is a sensible safety feature.

taking the first drive.

My own first test of an XK8 Coupe was with a car liberally endowed with optional equipment, amongst which were the Classic leather pack (a no-cost option including colour-co-ordinated trim and carpets, passenger seat height adjustment, burr walnut veneer, wood/leather steering wheel and wood gear knob), the memory pack

Digital readouts make way for navigation aid

(offering two preset positions for the driver's seat plus the reach and tilt of the steering column and the positions of the door mirrors), the navigation system (the screen for which replaced the three centre dials of

the standard instrument layout, whose information was relayed digitally instead) and steering wheel-mounted cruise control. At the time, these worthwhile extras added around £4,000 to the UK on the road price of the standard car of just under £51,000. A lot of money, but also a lot of car.

Accept that the XK8 Coupe is a car which essentially is a comfortable two-seater (with additional accommodation intended mainly for use in short-distance emergencies) and that its cockpit dimensions even in the front are not the most generous for a car of this overall size, and you have come close to exhausting the packaging shortcomings. The electric adjustment of seat and steering column, especially with the memory facility, makes light work of becoming comfortable and in command. The main instruments are quite deeply recessed, but you soon get used to reading them in a quick glance, though the centre control panel takes rather longer to master. If you include the audio and navigation equipment there are more than 40 different pressbuttons to play with and it takes a while to learn to hit the correct one each time. Fortunately, most of them are needed only rarely.

The most important controls are all well-placed. Whether you brake with the right or, as I do, the left foot, the generously large footrest to the left of the pedal is a sensible idea, while the handbrake's location alongside the driver's seat cushion is very convenient, especially as the lever drops down after use so as not to impede cockpit entry and exit. The J-gate transmission selector is comfortably within reach and the various positions well defined, and the control switch for selecting the sport (S) or normal mode is conveniently placed just behind it, alongside the master switch for the cruise control when fitted. The extra smoothness offered in the normal mode is

Sport setting preferred for open-road driving

ideal for boulevard cruising, but on the open road most people will want to select the sport setting for the additional rev range it offers in the intermediate gears and the significantly better response out of slow corners.

The steering is sensibly geared and although the generous power assistance

means that it feels just a little on the light side at low speeds, the extra weighting that comes into play with more vigorous cornering is welcome. You can feel it when the front wheels are having a hard time over poor surfaces, not by shocks through the column but rather by minor tremors at the wheel rim. For a car with such a slippery shape, external visibility from the driver's seat, once it has been set at the correct cushion height for the occupant, is excellent

Kickdown turns a gentle pussycat into a tiger

and this is a surprisingly easy car to position accurately.

It is also a car which responds well to a driver's change of mood. Driven in a docile manner it is a well behaved pussycat, quietly covering the miles with a minimum of throttle, a complete absence of fuss and with remarkable quietness – on smooth roads there is just a gentle background noise from the air conditioning, the faintest transmission hum accompanying a neutral throttle pedal, and the V8 engine barely audible. Then bring in the kickdown and an initial growl from the engine is followed by a

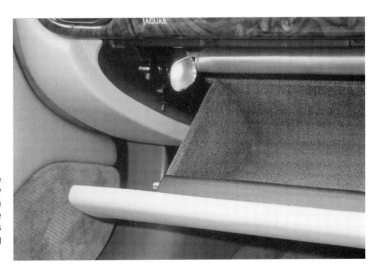

The useful-size glove compartment, illuminated by the light on the left, has an upper shelf into which the trimmed folder for the owner's handbook and supporting literature fits neatly.

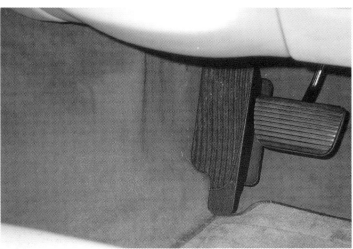

On cars fitted with the optional Memory Pack, the steering wheel automatically moves forwards and upwards to the tilt-away position as the ignition key is removed, then returns to its memorized position when the key is reinserted.

A substantial but detachable rest for the left foot is provided alongside the wide brake pedal, with a smaller rest hidden behind it for those who prefer this.

satisfying crescendo as the exhaust takes on a more musical note while the rev-counter needle sweeps rapidly round the dial. This really is a smooth power unit, one which is matched superbly to the transmission, the upshifts of which have such a silky quality that on occasions they really are imperceptible. Make use of the left side of the J-gate for a measure of manual control and you have that useful down-shifting facility for quick but safe progress into and through medium-speed corners. Less pleasing,

though, was the feel of the test car's brake pedal, which displayed a certain amount of sponginess through the early part of its travel before the hard work began, and a pedal pressure which was perhaps a little on the light side.

It has to be said that in some respects the XK8 is a frustrating car to drive, although this is not a criticism, but rather a condemnation of today's obsession by law enforcers with such unrealistically low speed limits even when away from rural and populated areas. Drive the XK8 at 40mph and it feels like 25, move the road speed on to 70mph and it feels more like 50, and what may well feel like 70mph behind the wheel will in fact have taken the needle up to around 90. All that performance, all that delightful music as the revs move into the upper segment of the dial, and yet so few places in which to enjoy it.

Nevertheless, the popularity of this Jaguar is easy to comprehend, for its virtues are numerous. The boot (trunk) is surprisingly roomy once you pull the oddments net aside and use its full depth. The quality of interior finish is of an entirely different class to what passed in Jaguars a few years ago, and no doubt durability too has vastly improved. It is a car which draws admiring glances whenever it is parked, and understandably so because it oozes style from every angle. A wonderful legacy to the late Geoff Lawson.

Climbing out of an XK8 and straight in behind the wheel of an XKR, especially one with some additional 'R' performance extras, was an interesting and revealing exercise. The second car was a Convertible, and with its firmer suspension settings and a set of optional BBS Detroit 20in wheels shod with ultra-low profile tyres it allowed a probing examination of the soft-top body's structural integrity. Inevitably, badly surfaced roads, of which there are a depressingly increasing number in urban areas of the UK, induce a

Shake resistance of Convertible well developed

certain amount of body shake, but nothing like the extent to which one might have anticipated. By all conventional standards this is a rigidly put together open-top car, far more shake-resistant than its predecessor in the XJS range. It was also interesting to discover that when driving with the top down, protection from the wind in the driver's seat was as effective with the door

Though quite deeply recessed, the main instruments have clear markings for rapid reading. Note that the red sector of the rev-counter begins at 6,800rpm, at which point the engine is well beyond its power peak.

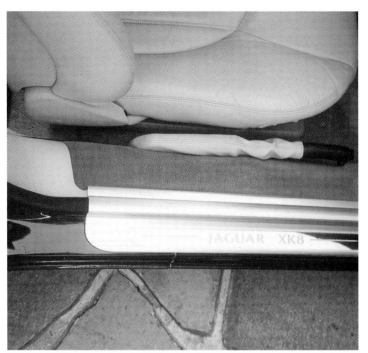

The handbrake drops to the floor after it has been engaged so as not to impede entry to or exit from the driver's seat.

windows lowered as with them raised.

The power-operated top is simplicity itself to lower, this being a one-button operation which releases the roof rail catch and also causes the rear quarter windows to disappear automatically, the button having to remain pressed throughout the operation. However, as its motors must consume a considerable amount of power, it seemed sensible to have the engine running, at least when raising the

Top raising and lowering performed with musical bell

top again. A discreet bell chimes to indicate the beginning and the end of the operation, but when the roof is being closed the second bell rings a few seconds before the quarter windows have raised themselves fully. Slipping the cover over a folded top is a simpler task than the meticulous

instructions in the handbook might indicate, but it is as well not to wait for the next shower of rain before raising the top because, of course, the cover has first to be detached and stowed carefully in its loose press-studded envelope which is carried in the boot (trunk).

Although significantly uprated compared with the XK8's settings, the XKR suspension retains more than adequate shock-absorption and even with the optional 20in BBS wheels and mix of '35%' front and '30%' rear tyres – which certainly enhance the car's steering

XKR performance aids safe overtaking on crowded roads

response – the ride quality is surprisingly good. This is a car which enjoys being driven hard, and the smooth surge of power from the supercharged engine is a delight, offering

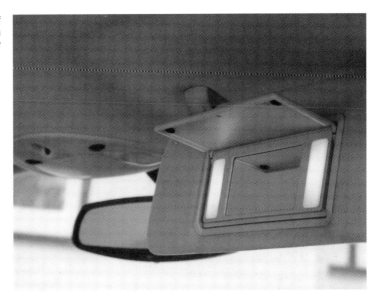

A hinged lid in the middle of each of the two sun visors can be lifted to expose a vanity mirror with side illumination.

the sort of vigorous and sustained acceleration which makes overtaking on crowded roads a safe and sure-footed manoeuvre, aided in no small measure by the reassuring feel of the very powerful Brembo brakes. Yet at low speeds the XKR retains the excellent flexibility and docility of the XK8; this really is a case of having the best of both worlds.

Whereas the Coupe might be accepted as a very occasional four-seater – or perhaps as a three-seater with the third person sitting with legs across the transmission tunnel – the Convertible is strictly for two people, and perhaps there is a case for a remodelled rear part of the cockpit, possibly offered as an option, which would replace the tiny seats with a properly furnished level platform to enhance this area's usefulness as additional storage space for luggage. Inevitably, the space needed to accommodate the furled top has impinged slightly on the capacity of the boot (trunk) as compared with the Coupe's.

Of course, the majority of XK8 or XKR buyers will have another vehicle for use when carrying capacity takes precedence over performance and style, the two areas in which these delightful Jaguars excel. They are not truly the sons of E-type – though in some respects they are a great deal more than that – but they have restored Jaguar's reputation as a highly respected manufacturer of sports cars of real quality, refinement and durability and have pointed the way towards other exciting new products which are destined to follow.

A coin tray recessed into the bottom of the facia panel is a convenient item. To the right of it are the release buttons for the fuel cap and trunk lid and above the tray the button for restricting access during valet parking.

This is how the electrically lowered top of the Convertible folds before the cover is attached manually.

Minimal foot room in the rear compartment of the Convertible means that this model effectively is a two-seater unless the people in the front are short in stature and the driver likes to be close to the wheel.

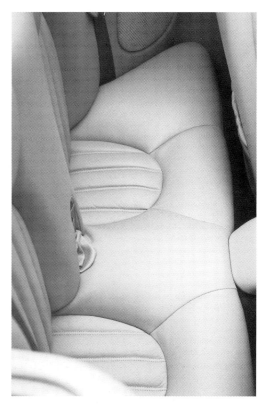

The space-saver spare wheel is distinctively painted bright red and carries clear markings indicating that 50mph (80km/h) is the maximum permissible speed during its temporary use.

Door windows up or down, the Convertible offers excellent protection from wind buffeting thanks to its carefully developed aerodynamics.

Concept styling, one of the most challenging yet rewarding tasks for members of Jaguar's Special Vehicle Operations' department.

CHAPTER 9

A LOOK INTO THE FUTURE

XK180 and F-type Concept

The design, development and productionizing of the XK8 and its XKR derivative, of which well over 50,000 have been sold in less than four years, is only the beginning of the story of Jaguar's return to the premium sports car arena. Many more exciting products are in the pipeline, as has been indicated by various concept and prototype vehicles which have appeared in public at recent motor shows and beyond the public's gaze on remote test tracks around the world.

The first of these to go on show, the Jaguar XK180, was a project conceived by the company's Special Vehicle Operations department and it had two primary functions. The first was to celebrate the 50th anniversary of the productionizing of the first XK sports car, the sublimely beautiful 1948 XK120 roadster, and to remind the world that half a century on Jaguar was as heavily committed as it had ever been to the concept of the refined sports two-seater. The second was to showcase the talents of the company's SVO staff, who were hard at work not only on producing bespoke versions of existing production models for their most affluent, discerning and discriminating customers, but also on developing high-performance 'add-on' products for existing and future model ranges, as either factory-fit options or dealer-fit accessories, to be marketed under the R Performance banner.

Based on the under-structure of an XKR Convertible, the XK180 was unveiled at the Paris motor show in September 1998, when Jaguar's people did their best to stress that this was nothing more than a concept car,

one that was most definitely *not* intended for production. Inevitably, of course, despite all the denials of intent to productionize it, the very existence of the XK180 provoked the question: 'How soon will I be able to buy one?', and the sales and marketing people had their work cut out convincing the questioners that when they said 'Never' they meant precisely that. The problem was, many people saw in the XK180 the shape of the car they had dreamed of for so long – the spiritual successor to the E-type – so their expectation that the car really *would* find its way into production one day, despite the official denials, was at least understandable.

But closer scrutiny should have convinced onlookers that this mouth-watering design was in fact something very different – a radical two-seater roadster which looked backwards as well as forwards and combined echoes not so much of the E-type as of the more spartan race-bred D-type. There were also some touches of the stillborn mid-engined XJ13 sports-racer and of the XJ220 supercar, plus some typical Jaguar-style luxury treatment and, beneath the aluminium skin, examples of the latest developments in modern technology. Almost a 21st Century version of the D-type-related XK SS, perhaps.

But the XK SS would never have been created had there not been kits of parts already in existence because of the fall-off in demand for the D-type; the rushed development of a road-going version was a convenient way of using these up, and of course all the fundamental engineering for the car had already been completed. To

Concept cars have long played a significant role in Jaguar's forward planning, but this is one that got away. The beautiful mid-engined XJ13 was virtually destroyed in a high-speed testing accident, but it has subsequently been painstakingly rebuilt and is now displayed as a reminder of what might have been.

productionize the XK180 would have meant virtually starting again from scratch – an immensely costly and time-consuming project, at the end of which would have emerged a car so expensive that the market for it would have been miniscule.

Meanwhile, the XK180 concept could at least be assessed as a worthy tribute to Jaguar's racing heritage, in some respects an intriguing glimpse into the future, perhaps, but most importantly as that required showcase of the skills and talents of Jaguar stylists, craftsmen and engineers, who in handling this project had managed to convert an idea into a drivable reality in just 42 weeks.

This was the first major ground-up project undertaken by Jaguar's SVO department, whose workshops in Browns Lane had come into being after production of the Daimler Limousine ended in the early-Nineties. Normally the department was filled by craftsmen engaged in producing those bespoke vehicles for affluent customers, for it is company policy that any Jaguar (or Daimler) model can be given the SVO treatment, which can range from a special paint or trim finish to mechanical upgrades and even to structural changes. So the creation of the XK180 represented quite a departure for the specialist workforce and, with such a tight timescale involved, a considerable challenge.

For the design team, the two major influences on the shape of the car were to be the stripped down XK120 which was taken to the Jabbeke motorway in Belgium in 1949 to prove that 120mph was well within the new roadster's reach (in fact test driver Ron Sutton had recorded 132.596mph over a flying mile) and the superbly styled D-type of Le Mans fame. But technically, the car would be derived from the supercharged XKR, a model which had yet to be revealed to the public.

During November 1998, principal designer Keith Helfet and SVO's principal engineer Gary Albrighton held preliminary discussions with the late Geoff Lawson – at that time Jaguar's chief stylist – and SVO manager Mike Massey, and they concluded that a shortened version of the XKR with a more powerful engine was a fitting basis on which to start the project. It was also decided that the XK180 would have an aluminium-panelled body, just as the original XK120 had

when it was first conceived as a limited-production roadster.

Helfet, who was also the stylist behind the shape of the XJ220, began sketching possible ideas on paper and computers, then set about designing the new body and converting it into a full-scale clay model. This began to take shape at Loades Design, a sister company of Abbey Panels – an old-established Coventry company whose collaboration with Jaguar goes back many years and includes supplying body panels for the C-type and D-type models, the XJ13 mid-engined prototype and the XJ220.

Meanwhile, within eight weeks the SVO engineers, working under Gary Albrighton, who became the XK180 project manager, had modified an XKR platform, 125mm (nearly 5 inches) being cut out of the cockpit area – the wheelbase therefore being reduced by the same amount – and provision made for shorter front and rear body sections. Overall, there would be a reduction in length of 345mm ($13\frac{1}{2}$in) compared with the XKR,

A symbolic shot of the XK180 at Silverstone with a D-type Jaguar, one of the cars which inspired it, in the background.

The XK180 and the XKR Convertible on which the Concept car was based. The two Jaguars are sharing sets of 20in diameter Paris wheels.

both front and rear overhangs being reduced by 110mm (nearly 4½in). Helfet's proposed body came out just 9mm wider than the XKR's, while the key windscreen/A-post datum point had been moved 100mm rearwards; the doors, which would have fixed glasses and no external handles – their release was to be by internal pull cords – were to be shortened by a similar amount. There was more than a trace of the racing heritage at the rear of the car, the upper part of the bodywork behind the cockpit being shaped into two tapering fairings behind robust looking twin roll-over bars.

By April 1999 the clay model design had been approved and detailed modifications were made to it before it was used to create the tooling aids and moulds from which the aluminium panels would be formed. Had the XK180 been a production model, the clay would have been digitized at this stage in order to create the tools, but as a one-off project this was not necessary.

Simultaneously, SVO created a separate 'cut and shut' XKR to act as a test 'mule' for the shorter and more powerful car. It was a purposeful evolution of the standard model and the fact that it was equipped with a full racing safety cage spoke volumes of the hard work which was ahead of it. With modifications to engine and suspension to test, plus different brakes, wheels and tyres to evaluate, much of this work had to take place off the highway, and many hours were spent pounding round both the high-speed track and the handling circuit at the test centre of the Motor Industry Research Association (MIRA), near Nuneaton.

The body tooling aids were ready during May and, working from formers and shapes created from the clay styling model, Abbey Panels' craftsmen began the task of panel forming, working entirely by traditional methods, rolling and shaping the components by hand and eye. By mid-June the body was ready for painting, and Helfet selected a colour which combined the metallic blue of the 1957 Le Mans-winning Ecurie Ecosse D-type with undertones of green and gold.

Right from the start of the project, Helfet was determined that any car which was to celebrate 50 years of XK heritage had to draw heavily on themes from the past – from the race track as well as the road – and nowhere was this to be seen more clearly than in the cockpit, where behind the double-bubble windshield, which blended smoothly into the tapering door glasses, the dashboard, in engine-turned aluminium, carried switches that echoed so clearly the style of the Le Mans Jaguars of the Fifties. Similar machined-turned aluminium sheet was used to cover the centre console and the door kickplates. But there were luxury touches, too, the Recaro seats being trimmed in cream and green Connolly leather, the three-spoke steering wheel also being leather-trimmed, and the carpets made from Ulster velvet, while 21st Century technology was to be found in the sequential gear selection by means of twin buttons on the steering wheel which supplemented the XKR's console-mounted J-gate, the shift lever of which had

to be moved left for control to be passed to the steering wheel buttons.

The large matching speedometer and rev-counter dials in front of the driver were supplemented by a row of five smaller circular dials stretching across the centre of the dashboard beneath a row of six toggle switches and above a quartet of warning lights. One of the small dials was a gear position indicator, a thoughtful addition for when the pushbutton controls (left button for up-shifts, right button for down-shifts) were in play.

It took four weeks to design the interior and a further two weeks to create the moulds that would be used to form the necessary panels. Meanwhile, trimmers more used to cushioning royalty and statesmen were hard at work on the racing seats and harnesses, and while the body men assembled the aluminium panels, the specially prepared AJ-V8 engine arrived from Whitley, along with some special chassis components which had been specified to fine-tune the handling. After two months of intense activity, the XK180 was ready to be photographed by mid-September, and after a further week on tiny detail jobs the car was ready to be

The installation of the uprated supercharged AJ-V8 engine in the XK180. A 10% increase in boost pressure and associated modifications enabled peak power to reach the development target of 450bhp.

The cockpit of the XK180. The J-gate was modified so as to be linked to press-button shift controls on the steering wheel, to activate which the J-gate lever has first to be pulled backwards and to the left.

transported to Paris.

Just as XK120 had indicated the speed potential of the 1949 roadster, so XK180 was an appropriate designation for the new concept car, especially as this was to be not merely a show exhibit, but a fully functional car to be driven and to perform in the manner in which its appearance suggested it should; with a final-drive ratio raised to 2.88:1 this was going to be a very fast car.

Development of the XKR's supercharged 4-litre engine began with the decision to raise the speed of the supercharger 10 per cent by increasing the drive ratio from 2:1 to 2.2:1. This, combined with increased airflow through the induction system with the help of different ducting and air cleaner, and a larger-bore exhaust system with straight-through silencers and no catalyst, enabled the maximum power figure to reach its target of 450bhp, 80bhp more than the engines installed in the production XKRs, while maximum torque was increased from 387 to 445lb.ft. These changes called for a larger intercooler, the radiator surface area being increased by 81 per cent, and a repiped split circuit with twin pumps.

The suspension of the XK180 was developed within SVO with assistance from the ride and handling experts at the Whitley Engineering Centre. Although based on that of the XKR, Bilstein competition-style aluminium shock absorbers were incorporated within the fully adjustable coil spring/damper units, the top mounts for which having been redesigned, while the rollbar linkages were extended and made fully adjustable, the rod ends being solid, and the ECU for the steering was retuned. Compared with the XKR, the XK180 sat 20mm closer to the ground. The Brembo braking system operated through aluminium four-pot calipers against 355mm x 32mm cross-drilled ventilated front discs and 315mm x 28mm similarly cross-drilled and ventilated discs at the rear. At that time the uniquely styled two-piece aluminium wheels were the largest yet to be fitted to a Jaguar. The rims were 20 inches in diameter and 9 inches wide at the front and 10 inches wide at the rear, the Pirelli P-Zero tyres being directional 255/35 ZR20s at the front and assymetrical 285/30 ZR20s at the rear.

A second XK180 was built, and this car, finished in slightly different exterior and trim colours and with left-hand drive, was exhibited at the 1999 North American International Auto Show in Detroit, where for the second time in three months Jaguar people were confronted by an avalanche of 'When can I buy one?' inquiries. Partly these were provoked by the knowledge that the two vehicles, far from being just static show exhibits, were already drivable cars. But the purpose behind this was that they should be

Testing reveals need for extra aerodynamic aids

used in addition to the earlier 'mule' to test components destined to find their way into future Jaguar models, as well as SVO-engineered upgrades to existing ones.

It was only when this testing process began in the UK that consideration was given to the XK180's aerodynamic performance, and after some initial test runs there were some early running changes, including the fitment of a deeper front spoiler, as well as a larger rear wing and a full-length undertray, while the driver's seating position was lowered.

But of course by this time the XK180 also had another hidden agenda. The tremendous enthusiasm with which it had been greeted on both sides of the Atlantic was clear enough evidence for Jaguar's product planners that something along similar lines, if productionized to sell at a competitive price, would find a mass of buyers. It really was time to think seriously of bringing to market a roadster, a true E-type successor.

But an F-type – if that was what it would be called – had to be a car unconstrained as the XK180 had been by being based on the structure of an existing model. It could borrow elements of the style of the XK180, and a lot of the mechanical goodies, too, but it would have to be not just a new model, but

F-type Concept less constrained than XK180

a new range of models, spanning a wide segment of the sports car market, and able to share componentry with both the S-class intermediate-size and the forthcoming smaller saloon (sedan) models, coded X400.

With an eye firmly on their most

The XK180 in profile. Note the tail wing and how the fuel filler has been neatly let into one of the two fairings behind the cockpit.

In some respects the XK180 represented a halfway house to the F-type Concept, which was able to be built on a shorter-wheelbase platform and styled with reduced front and rear overhangs.

The cockpit of the F-type Concept – functional, yet elegant in a minimalist way.

important sports car market, Jaguar chose the 2000 North American International Auto Show in Detroit as the launching pad for the F-type Concept, and this time there was no camouflaging the company's aim to bring this car, or something very closely related to it, to market. Jonathan Browning, Jaguar's managing director, said at the reveal: 'The F-type Concept roadster is an exercise in pure Jaguar sports car design. Its purpose is quite simply to provoke reaction from current and potential customers.'

A significantly more compact car than the XK180, the F-type Concept is 645mm (25in) shorter than the XKR on which the XK180 was based and is 100mm (4in) narrower than both cars. Although the design team led by Keith Helfet had begun work under the guidance of the late Geoff Lawson, who tragically died suddenly in June 1999, the project was completed by Ian Callum, who succeeded him as director of design and paid this tribute to his predecessor at the time of the car's launch: 'Sadly this car is the last to

bear Geoff's inimitable stamp. It is a fine example of the standards we will strive to maintain.'

Setting out to produce a shape that is contemporary, functional and distinctively

Equal weight distribution a design priority

Jaguar, the design team needed to fulfil Jaguar's core engineering value of equal weight distribution for optimum dynamic performance, so the concept dictated both a long bonnet and a cockpit which sits in the ideal position relative to the wheelbase. The

The oval air intake, so redolent of famous Jaguars of the past, works in conjunction with a full-width spoiler beneath.

design achieves the balanced proportions of a traditional Jaguar sports car, evocative of the seminal E-type, although Helfet was determined that the car should have its own

Speed-adjustable front aerofoil to increase downforce

personality and not become a pastiche of the Sixties design. 'Designing-in the Jaguar style is an instinctive process', he said.

Just as the E-type was one of the first mass-production cars to be shaped by aerodynamics, the F-type concept also features aerodynamic aids, including a 'splitter' in the nose of the car, a low-set aerofoil being designed to move automatically so as to increase downforce as the speed rises, while at the rear a fixed diffuser tunnel also achieves additional downforce as the speed increases.

The distinctively styled headlamps employ an adaptation of the latest Baroptic light guide technology in a unique multi-element cluster, while the ultra-compact rear lamps, pioneered in the XK180, use LED (Light Emitting Diode) technology to deliver high performance and a jewel-like appearance.

The interior, much of the detail of which was the responsibility of Adam Hatton and Pasi Pennanen, working under Helfet, is similar to that of the XK180, but it has also been inspired by the functional simplicity of the Lightweight E-type racer. The switches and cockpit fittings are fashioned from solid aluminium to provide a precision-engineered tactile quality.

There is no disguising that the underbody of the F-type Concept performs an important aerodynamic function, especially the diffuser at the rear of the car.

The pronounced curvature of the front and side screens suggests weather protection of the highest order. Note the high-mounted rear-view mirrors.

Most important for potential buyers, the F-type Concept does not sacrifice practicality for appearance, and the packaging, construction, accommodation, luggage space and worldwide legal requirements were all considered during its creation, as was the need to make the car production-ready without sacrificing its roadster spirit.

The car is designed to accept a range of powertrain options, starting with the 240bhp AJ-V6 engine used in the S-type saloon (sedan) models, while a supercharged version with around 300bhp is also a possibility. A choice of automatic or manual transmission has been provided for, driving the rear wheels, while all-wheel drive would also be feasible in production. The surest sign that the F-type is on its way came from Jonathan Browning when he said: 'The F-type Concept is a clear signal of Jaguar's intent to return to the true sports car market in which we were so successful in the 1950s and 60s. Complementing the recently launched S-type compact saloon and, next year (2001) the new X400 small saloon, the F-type Concept would attract a new generation of younger sports car buyers, both male and female, to the Jaguar marque.'

Slotting into the catalogue alongside the XK8 and XKR Coupes and Convertibles, a range of F-types will mean that by 2003 Jaguar will be more strongly represented in every segment of the sports car market than at any time in its history.

The shape of things to come?

APPENDIX A
TECHNICAL SPECIFICATIONS

Jaguar XK8 Coupe

Engine: 3,996cc (243.9cu in) 90deg V8-cylinder, 86mm (3.386in) bore x 86mm (3.386in) stroke, with aluminium block and cylinder heads. Twin chain-driven overhead camshafts per cylinder bank operating four valves per cylinder in pent-roof combustion chambers. Nippondenso engine management ECU controls electronic multi-point fuel injection and ignition, variable inlet cam phasing, and activates Stability Control and Traction Control when switched on. Compression ratio 10.75:1. Maximum power 290bhp (216kW) at 6,100rpm, maximum torque 290lb.ft (393Nm) at 4,250rpm.

Drivetrain: ZF 5HP24 fully electronic 5-speed automatic transmission; ratios 3.57:1, 2.20:1, 1.51:1, 1.00:1, 0.80:1, reverse 4.10:1. Final-drive ratio 3.06:1, 32mph per 1,000rpm in top gear.

Suspension: Fully independent. Front: unequal-length upper and lower wishbones with co-axial coil springs and telescopic dampers. Anti-roll bar and anti-dive under braking. Rear: lower wishbones with drive-shafts providing upper links, co-axial coil springs and telescopic dampers. Anti-roll bar and anti-squat and anti-lift under acceleration and braking. Optional Computer Active Technology Suspension (CATS) with uprated springs, adaptive damping and 18in wheels *(see below)*.

Steering: ZF Servotronic rack and pinion system with variable-ratio rack; 2.8 turns lock to lock.
Brakes: Teves vacuum-assisted system incorporating ABS with ventilated discs, 28mm x 305mm, front and rear.

Wheels and tyres: Alloy 5-spoke 8J x 17in wheels with Pirelli P Zero 245/50 ZR17 tyres with assymetric treads. Optional with CATS sports suspension: 7-spoke 8J x 18in wheels with Pirelli P-Zero 245/45 ZR18 directional front tyres and 255/45 assymetric-tread rear tyres, and 3.5J x 18in space-saver spare wheel with 135/80 R18 tyre.

Dimensions: Overall length 4,760mm (15ft 7.4in), overall width 1,829mm (6ft 0in), including mirrors 2,015mm (6ft 7.3in), overall height 1,296mm (4ft 3in), wheelbase 2,588mm (8ft 5.9in), front track 1,504mm (4ft 11.2in), rear track 1,498mm (4ft 11in). Fuel tank capacity 75 litres (16.5 Imperial, 19.9 US gallons). Luggage trunk capacity 327 litres (11.5cu ft). Kerb weight 1,615kg (3,560lb).

Jaguar XK8 Convertible

As for Jaguar XK8 Coupe except:
Suspension: CATS option not available until September 1997.
Dimensions: Overall height 1,306mm (4ft 3.4in). Luggage truck capacity 307 litres (10.8cu ft). Kerb weight 1,705kg (3,756lb).

Jaguar XKR Coupe and Convertible

As for Jaguar XK8 Coupe and Convertible except:

Engine: Equipped with Eaton M112 supercharger operating at 10-12psi boost pressure. Supercharger ratio 2:1. Maximum power 370bhp (276kW) at 6,150rpm, maximum torque 387lb.ft (535Nm) at 3,600rpm. Addition of intercooler radiator.

Drivetrain: Mercedes-Benz WA580 fully electronic 5-speed automatic transmission; ratios 3.59:1, 2.19:1, 1.41:1, 1.00:1, 0.83:1.

Suspension: Recalibrated CATS package standard equipment. Revised spring rates, roll bars and damper settings.

Steering: Revised valve settings for Servotronic rack and stiffer rack mounts.

Wheels and tyres: BBS alloy 10-spoke split-rim 8J x 18in front and 9J x 18in rear wheels with Pirelli P-Zero 245/45 ZR18 directional front and 255/45 ZR18 assymetric rear tyres.

Dimensions: Kerb weights: Coupe 1,640kg (3,614lb), Convertible 1,750kg (3,857kg).

Jaguar XKR Silverstone Coupe and Convertible
As for Jaguar XKR Coupe and Convertible except:
Suspension: Coupe equipped with Handling Kit incorporating uprated springs and anti-roll bars front and rear and lowered ride height.

Brakes: Brembo system with 4-piston aluminium calipers, two-piece 335 x 32mm front discs, single-piece 330 x 28mm rear discs, ventilated and cross-drilled.

Wheels and tyres: BBS Detroit 5-spoke split-rim 9J x 20in front and 10J x 20in rear wheels with Pirelli P-Zero 255/35 ZR20 directional front and 285/30 ZR20 assymetric rear tyres.

Jaguar XK180 Concept
As for Jaguar XKR Convertible except:
Engine: Supercharger gearing changed from 2:1 to 2.2:1. Maximum power 450bhp, maximum torque approx 445lb.ft..

Drivetrain: Gearshift via J-gate or steering wheel-mounted buttons.

Brakes: Cross-drilled ventilated discs, 355mm front, 315mm rear.

Wheels and tyres: Pirelli P-Zero 255/35 ZR20 directional front and 285/30 ZR20 assymetric rear tyres.

Dimensions: Overall length 4,635mm (15ft 2.5in), overall width 2,015mm (6ft 7.3in), overall height 1,285mm (4ft 2.6in), wheelbase 2,460mm (8ft 0.85in). Kerb weight 1,560kg (3,438lb).

Jaguar F-type Concept
Preliminary details as for Jaguar XK180 except:
Dimensions: Overall length 4,115mm (7ft 10.5in), overall width 1,732mm (5ft 8.25in), overall height 1,090mm (3ft 7.0in), wheelbase 2,400mm (7ft 10.5in).

APPENDIX B
XK-SERIES SALES FIGURES BY YEAR AND MARKET

Market	Body style	1996	1997	1998	1999	2000*
UK	Coupe	563	1534	1837	1036	629
	Convertible	382	1283	1076	876	512
North America	Coupe	482	1129	767	590	580
	Convertible	1701	6094	5422	5859	3725
Europe	Coupe	465	1828	1691	1430	920
	Convertible	324	1584	1519	1602	1031
Other overseas	Coupe	239	721	408	291	162
	Convertible	117	328	199	156	82
Total sales	Coupe	1749	5212	4703	3347	2291
	Convertible	2524	9289	8216	8493	5350
	All models	**4273**	**14501**	**12919**	**11840**	**7641**

* Year 2000 figures to end of July only.

These sales figures reveal the following interesting statistics:

+ Overall, Convertibles have out-sold Coupes by approximately 2 to 1.

+ In North America Convertibles have out-sold Coupes by over 6.4 to 1.

+ In all other markets Coupes have out-sold Convertibles by 1.24 to 1.

+ North America has accounted for 51.5% of all XK sales.

+ Continental Europe has accounted for 24.2% of sales.

+ The UK market as accounted for 19.0% of sales.

+ The rest of the world has accounted for the remaining 5.3% of sales.

APPENDIX C
XK8 AND XKR PRODUCTION FIGURES

XK8 Coupe and Convertible

Coupe	JAN	FEB	MAR	APR	MAY	JUN	JUL	AUG	SEP	OCT	NOV	DEC	YEAR
1996	2	5	11	10	45	244	106	467	567	609	422	437	**2925**
1997	622	527	613	778	293	380	231	255	285	394	397	366	**5141**
1998	396	367	325	406	197	247	120	234	242	289	263	233	**3319**
1999	146	124	110	72	119	147	72	121	201	212	184	193	**1701**
2000	179	162	114	77	147	116	72	110					**977**
Conv													
1996	2	2	12	2	62	42	314	699	848	912	636	656	**4187**
1997	934	791	918	1165	868	1140	693	774	732	603	593	554	**9765**
1998	586	585	632	743	518	734	369	691	664	783	704	653	**7662**
1999	565	556	753	519	566	599	311	382	491	507	498	449	**6196**
2000	469	385	610	392	549	522	371	332					**3630***

XKR Coupe and Convertible

Coupe	JAN	FEB	MAR	APR	MAY	JUN	JUL	AUG	SEP	OCT	NOV	DEC	YEAR
1997	–	–	–	–	–	–	–	–	3	2	5	–	**10**
1998	4	38	149	136	116	152	91	155	139	152	129	141	**1402**
1999	105	122	199	152	119	102	54	86	139	147	167	138	**1530**
2000	127	164	201	145	138	128	128	138					**1169**
Conv													
1997	–	–	–	–	–	–	–	–	3	2	6	2	**13**
1998	6	21	79	70	58	84	54	85	96	107	83	95	**838**
1999	177	184	178	145	137	142	68	109	192	208	240	214	**1994**
2000	150	267	313	268	249	223	225	273					**1968***

*Year 2000 figures to end of August only.

Production totals by model and year

Model	1996	1997	1998	1999	2000*	Total
XK8 Coupe	2925	5141	3319	1701	977	**14063**
XK8 Convertible	4187	9765	7662	6196	3630	**31440**
XKR Coupe	–	10	1402	1530	1169	**4111**
XKR Convertible	–	13	838	1994	1968	**4813**
All models	**7112**	**14929**	**13221**	**11421**	**7744**	**54427**

* To end of August.

APPENDIX D
XK8 AND XKR PERFORMANCE FIGURES

	XK8 *Autocar*	XK8 *Road & Track*	XKR* *Car and Driver*	XKR *Car and Driver*
Mean max speed (mph)**	155	156	155	155
0-30mph (sec)	2.3	2.5	1.9	2.1
0-40mph	3.4	3.5	2.7	2.9
0-50mph	4.9	4.9	3.7	4.0
0-60mph	6.6	6.4	4.9	5.2
0-70mph	8.4	8.2	6.2	6.6
0-80mph	10.7	10.3	7.9	8.3
0-90mph	13.5	12.8	9.8	10.3
0-100mph	16.7	15.7	12.0	12.5
0-110mph	20.5	–	14.6	15.3
0-120mph	27.1	–	18.2	19.0
Standing 1/4 mile	15.2	14.8	13.5	13.8
10-30mph	2.1	–	–	–
20-40mph	2.2	–	–	–
30-50mph	2.6	–	2.7	2.8
40-60mph	3.2	–	–	–
50-70mph	3.5	–	3.2	3.3
60-80mph	4.1	–	–	–
70-90mph	5.1	–	–	–
80-100mph	6.0	–	–	–
90-110mph	7.0	–	–	–
100-120mph	10.4	–	–	–
Typical mpg	22.9	20.1	21.0 (US)	18.0(US)
Kerb weight (kg)	1,653	1,653	1,709	1,725
Year tested	1996	1996	1998	2000

* European-specification car tested in England

** Top speed electronically limited